COPING
W H E N

A Parent

Goes Back

to Work

Gwen K. Packard

THE ROSEN PUBLISHING GROUP, INC./NEW YORK

Published in 1995 by The Rosen Publishing Group, Inc.
29 East 21st Street, New York, NY 10010

First Edition

Library of Congress Cataloging-in-Publication Data

Packard, Gwen K.
    Coping when a parent goes back to work / Gwen K. Packard.
       p.   cm.
    Includes bibliographical references and index.
    ISBN 0-8239-1698-7
    1. Working mothers—Juvenile literature.   2. Work and family—Juvenile literature.   3. Family—Juvenile literature.
    [1. Work and family.   2. Working mothers.   3. Family life.]
    I. Title.
    HQ759.48.P33   1994
    306.874—dc20
                                                        94-13198
                                                             CIP
                                                              AC

Manufactured in the United States of America

When Mr. Foster was finally able to work full time, Mack was upset. He was surprised at his own reaction. "I guess I just got used to having Dad around the house. It was a real jolt when he went back to work. Mom continued to work longer hours, because we still needed the extra money."

EMOTIONAL NEEDS

Although many mothers go back to work because of financial need, your mother may choose to get a job for more personal, or emotional, reasons. Your mother may feel that she has never developed her own identity, as she has never been on her own. She may feel that she is not appreciated, and she understands that working outside the home often helps build self-esteem.

Mothers need to get out of the house. They have a need for independence and a desire to have their own identity outside of the family and the house. Because you, as a teenager, are seeking independence and personal identity, you can understand this need. Boys and girls support the idea of their mothers going back to work.

Sixteen-year-old Zoe was not exactly sure about all the reasons why her mom wanted to have a job. But she understood that her mom needed something of her own, her own identity.

When twins Vic and Linda started high school, their mother was bored staying alone at home all day. "It used to be pretty chaotic for Mom, having twins around all the time," Linda says, laughing. "We're not home much now. It's just too quiet for Mom. We all know she'll be a happier person if she goes back to work."

As Marie Kraft and her younger brother Danny were growing up, their mother stayed home to take care of them and the house. After Danny entered first grade, their mother became a volunteer in the schools as a reading tutor and teacher's aide. She worked so many hours that it was almost like a full-time job. When Marie was in high school and Danny was in junior high, their mother announced that she wanted to go back to work at a full-time job.

Marie was confused. "You're already working, Mom. Why do you need a full-time job?" she asked.

Before his mother could answer, Danny said, "Mom's not really working. She's not getting paid."

"That's the point," Mrs. Kraft said. "That's the way most people think. There is little respect for unpaid work. I need a paying full-time job for my self-esteem. Besides, I'm volunteered out. I want to do something else now."

Your mother may have been very happy staying home with her children and taking care of the house. Many mothers are. But as the children grow older and become more independent, that is the time mothers consider going back to work.

Tyrell and Azi Jennings's mother thought that staying home when her children were little was the right thing to do. But, their mother also *wanted* to stay home. It was a personal choice. She enjoyed taking care of the family and the household, and for years she did not consider working outside the home.

Eventually, Tyrell and Azi's mom could see that her teenage children didn't need her to be at home as much. "I was tired of looking for tennis games and going to shopping malls," Mrs. Jennings says. "I decided to go back to school to get my college degree, and then go to work in the business world."

Another emotional reason for a mother to choose to go back to work may be a need to get away from a conflict at home. If there is conflict in the marriage, or tension between parent and child, a parent may be able to ease that stress by going to work outside the home.

If your mother has been on welfare for many years, she probably wants to go back to work for both emotional and financial reasons.

John Martin was three and his sister Jill was just a baby when their father left their mother. Mrs. Martin had never worked outside the home. Although she had a high school diploma, she had no skills to qualify her for a well-paying job. She also felt that she could not leave her two little children in order to work. So Mrs. Martin applied for welfare.

As John and Jill grew up, their mother was always at home to take care of them. The welfare money did not buy much. Mrs. Martin often talked about getting a job so they would have more money and a better life, but she didn't know where to begin.

One day, when John was thirteen, his mother learned from the church pastor that a new program was being set up in the neighborhood. A manufacturing firm and a county agency working together were going to train a small group of welfare mothers for positions in the company. The mothers would then be eligible to get good jobs with the company.

John, Jill, and their mother discussed the idea. Mrs. Martin told her children that if she took the training and then got the job, she would not be home during the day to take care of them, and she would not have time to do all the things at home that she was doing now. They would have to help with the housework, laundry, and meals.

"I've wanted to go to work for a long time, and this is my chance," Mrs. Martin said. "I will make a lot more money than welfare pays me. We can buy better food and more of it. We can buy some clothes for the two of you, and maybe a few toys and games."

John wasn't sure he liked the idea. He was used to having his mom around. He didn't want to do all the things his mother would expect him to do; he wasn't ready to accept so much responsibility. But when John saw how enthusiastic his mother was about the idea, he changed his opinion. John could see that his mother had both emotional and financial reasons for going back to work.

DISCUSSING REASONS

No matter what the situation, ask your parent to explain why he or she is going back to work. You need to talk about what changes are going to take place, how they will affect you, and how you can adjust to those changes. Everyone in the family should express their opinions and contribute to the discussion.

If your mother goes back to work by choice rather than necessity, you and your family will probably have more time for planning. Your mother has more options when there is no financial emergency, and there is more time to consider those options. She may decide to work part time at first. Or, she may choose to go back to school part time before taking a full-time job.

After doing volunteer work for many years, Tam Long's mother wanted to work full time. Fifteen-year-old Tam, his mother and father, and his younger sister Mai, had many discussions about the idea.

Mrs. Long discussed the reasons she want to work. Now that Tam was in high school, and Mai was starting junior high, she knew she would want to do more than just stay home and take care of the house.

Tam, his sister, and father expressed their opinions, most of them negative. "You won't be here when I get home from school," Mai said.

"Who's going to cook dinner?" Tam wondered.

"What about all the shopping and cleaning?" Mr. Long added.

"We'll do a lot of planning. And, of course, everyone will help," Mrs. Long said. The two kids and their dad looked at each other and groaned.

One evening after dinner, later that week, Tam's mother announced, "I know many families like ours where the mother has gone back to work full time, and things run pretty smoothly. But I can see from our discussions that it's not going to work out that easily for our family. I'm not giving up on the idea of working, but I'm willing to compromise, if you will, too.

"I've decided to start working part time, instead of full time. Maybe after a few years the situation will change, and I can switch to a full-time job. But I still expect everyone to help," Mrs. Long added emphatically. This time there were no groans.

Not every mother will alter her plans if there are negative opinions in her family. Whether it is for financial, emotional, or other reasons, your mother's need to work full time may be so strong that she must go ahead over all objections.

CHAPTER 2

I'm Not Sure I'm Going to Like This

When you first learn that your mom or dad is going back to work, you will probably have many conflicting emotions, both positive and negative. Whether or not your parents discussed the situation with you before they made their decision, you can expect to have a variety of emotions. You may even become angry and feel deserted. You may feel fearful, uncertain, disappointed, or frustrated. You may be asking yourself, "What's going to happen to me?"

It may be that your mom has always been available and ready to do things for you, especially if she has not worked outside of home since you were born. She may always have been there to help you with your homework, or to drive you to activities or friends' houses.

If this is how it's been, you are definitely going to notice a difference when your mom goes back to work. Suddenly, your mom won't be as available as she once was. You'll miss having her around and miss all the things she used to do for you.

If your father goes back to work after having been unemployed or working at home for a long time, you'll have the same sense of loss.

The initial reactions of teenagers to parents going back to work differs from family to family and even among the members of one family. Emotions range from enthusiasm to hostility, with many shades in between.

When Becky was a junior in high school, her mother went back to work. Becky was excited about it. Because her mom had always wanted Becky to go to college and have a career, Becky figured that was what her mother wanted for herself, too. Her mother had a career and was working before Becky was born. For many years, Becky's mother had planned to go back to work when her children were old enough.

"I think it's great that Mom is going back to work," Becky told a friend. "It's not going to make a big difference to me. I have so many school activities, Mom hardly ever sees me before dinner time, anyway."

Becky's younger brothers had different reactions. Her brother Ted was in high school, too, but he didn't have as many school activities as Becky. He had projects that he liked to work on at home. Ted was happy to hear that his mother was going to work. That will give me more time to myself, he thought.

Becky's youngest brother, Andrew, was worried about his mother working. How would he get along without her? he wondered. Would he have to be home by himself a lot? Andrew felt better when his mother explained that there would always be someone at home when he came home from school. Sometimes that person would be Becky or Ted, and sometimes it would be Andrew's grandmother.

When Carl Richardson's mother first told her family

she was planning to go back to work, Carl became very negative. Carl was thirteen at the time. He felt anger, fear, and confusion all at once. He couldn't understand why his mother would want to go to work. He was most unhappy because his mother's job would take her time and attention away from him.

Carl took it out on his mother by being hostile. He was quarrelsome, refused to do his regular household chores, and tried to hurt his mother by telling her she would not succeed. The situation was made even worse for Carl's mother because his father had the same attitude.

The only bright spot for Mrs. Richardson was the attitude of her daughter, Chris, who was two years older than Carl. Chris was actually happy that her mother got a job. She realized that her mother had done a lot for the family and had made a lot of sacrifices. She was sure that if her mother wanted to work outside the home, that would make her mother happy.

Mrs. Richardson was grateful that her daughter agreed. She tried to convince her husband and son that things would work out. In fact, she felt that her working would be a benefit to the family because she would be a happier and more interesting person. After a while, her husband's and son's attitudes did soften a little.

Mrs. Richardson was determined to go to work. She felt it was something she had to do. She hoped that eventually her whole family would accept her decision, but she had to go forward with her plans in either case.

Eventually, Mrs. Richardson encouraged her family to visit a therapist with her. The therapist helped them to sort out their feelings, and Carl and his father came to understand that their hostility arose from their own feelings of insecurity. Through the family therapy, they were able to get rid of these immature feelings and grew to be very proud of Mrs. Richardson's abilities and the fact that she had a job.

Fifteen-year-old Ben Barclay was also hostile toward the idea of his mother's going back to work. It had only been two months since his parents had a big argument and his mother told his father to get out of the house. Then his mother filed for divorce.

Ben felt sorry for his dad. How could his mother tell him to leave? Ben remembered the good things about his dad and seemed to forget the bad things. But Mrs. Barclay had to demand that her husband leave because he had hit her, and such behavior should never be accepted.

When his mother went back to work, Ben's anger increased. "If Dad was still around, you wouldn't have to go to work," he yelled at his mother.

"If he was still here, things would be much worse," his mother answered. "You yourself said you couldn't stand living with a person who was abusive. Think about all the problems he caused. Compared to that, my going back to work is a minor problem that we can work out. Having our own money will enable us to do the things that we need to do for ourselves."

Unlike Carl and Ben, Scott and Steven were enthusiastic about their mother's decision to go back to work. Mrs. Conway had stayed home until her two sons were in junior high school.

The family were vacationing at EPCOT Center. As they walked from one exhibit to another, Mrs. Conway saw a sign that read, "If you dream it, you can do it."

"That became my motto. It started me thinking about what I would like to do with my life," Mrs. Conway said.

"Perhaps the idea was in the back of my mind for a long time," Mrs. Conway continued. "But it just popped up one day. I decided I wanted to finish college and then go to work. I called my husband, and he said, 'Go for it!' Scott and Steven were happy about it because they realized that this would make me happy. There were many people who doubted whether I would succeed, but not my family."

When Jim's parents first told him that his mother was going to work, he had a variety of emotions and a lot of questions. He was surprised. He told some of his friends he was "shocked." He had no idea this was going to happen, because his mother hadn't said anything before. He was angry.

Even though his parents offered to discuss the issue with him, Jim knew the matter was already settled. They had planned things without telling him and without asking him what he thought about it first. What good would discussing it do?

Although he wouldn't admit this to anyone else, Jim was scared, too. What's going to happen to me? Jim asked himself. Am I just going to be suddenly abandoned? If Mom isn't around, who's going to do the cooking and the laundry and all those other things Mom always did? What's the matter with Mom, doesn't she like being a mother any more? Doesn't she like *me* any more?

Jim decided to be cool. On the outside, he acted as if he didn't care. "I don't need Mom around any more," he said out loud.

Finally, Jim agreed to discuss the matter with his parents. He still wasn't going to tell them how he really felt. After dinner one evening, Jim and his parents sat around the dining room table to talk. Jim's mother explained why she had decided to go back to work. It was partly because they needed money to send Jim to college, and partly because Jim didn't need his mother around so much. She needed something more fulfilling in her life.

"I didn't discuss it with you before I made the decision because it was a very personal choice," Jim's mom said. "This was one of the few times I had to decide for myself. No one else could do it for me."

Jim's parents explained that Jim would have to take responsibility for some of the things his mother once did. Jim certainly was old enough and capable of helping. Because his mom wouldn't start work for two weeks, there was time to plan how household chores and other activities would be taken care of.

"Don't worry or think you're being abandoned," Jim's dad said. "Mom will still be here for you. And don't forget about me. I'm going to share more of the house-work, and I'll be here for you, too."

By the time the family had finished the discussion, Jim's feelings of anger and fear had decreased. He understood that his mother would be happier. Of course, that made him happy, too, but the whole idea would take some getting used to.

The more a family talks and plans, the better. Whether you have a single parent, or you're living with both parents, try to have a family meeting. Everyone in your family—adults, teens, and younger children—should know what to expect. They should also know what is expected of them.

You can help with the planning if you ask yourself the following questions:

- What can I do for myself when my parent goes back to work?
- What can I do for my parents?
- What do I want my parents to do for me?

There should be an opportunity for you to voice your opinion. Your ideas may make the transition easier. Your parents should tell you what can be negotiated and what cannot. For instance, you cannot tell your mother not to go to work, but you may be able to negotiate what you do with your spare time.

Your anger, fear, and frustration can be reduced when you plan with your parent. As far in advance as possible before the new job starts, your family should discuss the changing family roles.

CHAPTER 3

Changing Family Roles

So now you know your parent is going back to work. You expect changes to take place in your life. Most of those changes—and the biggest ones—will happen right at home.

When both your parents are working—or if your single parent is working—the role each member of the family plays will change. The position of each person in the family, what they do, and their relationships with the other members of the family are going to change.

You may have to do things for yourself that your parents did for you in the past. You may begin doing things for your parents that they once did for themselves. As the teenager in the family, you may have more tasks than younger family members. You may have to care for younger sisters and brothers, do laundry, run errands, go grocery shopping, prepare meals, and clean house.

The number of changes you experience, and the way you feel about those changes, will depend on the amount of responsibility you had before your parent went back to work. Was it your job to make your own bed, help with meals, do the dishes, or care for younger brothers and sisters before your parent went back to work? Or did Mom and Dad do a lot of those things for you? In that case, you will feel a big change in your life, if those jobs suddenly become your responsibility.

Believe it or not, your mother may have an even harder time getting used to her new role than you do. It is new to her that others in the family will be doing the housework that she has always done. In the beginning, she may still try to do most of the work around the house. She may be afraid that someone else won't do the job right. You should offer to share the work, and you should reassure your mother that you can be depended upon to do the job right.

PLANNING

When a parent goes back to work, there should be more planning and cooperation than there was in the past. Everyone should take part in the planning process. It might be a new experience for your parents, but they will have to delegate work to each member of the family. A good plan starts with a family meeting.

The Planning Meeting

"At first I thought my parents were kidding when they said they were going to have a family meeting," fifteen-year-old Debbie says. "They wanted to plan how we were going to do things around the house after Mom went back to work. They wanted everyone to participate.

"I didn't know what to expect. I mean, we've never had

a family meeting before. But Mom and Dad were ready. They had a pretty good idea of what needed to be taken care of around the house and how to assign the chores.

"They wanted everyone to take part and share their ideas, even my younger brother Keith and my little sister Sherry. They wanted to know what jobs each one wanted to do, even though you would have to do more than just those things. Keith said he would be the official TV watcher and video game player. He's such a comedian.

"But the meeting was okay. Before we started planning, I was really worried that I would be given all the house-work and cooking, and the baby-sitting, too. What could a twelve-year-old and an eight-year-old do? Well, I found out they can do a lot of things, including helping with the housework and the cooking.

"We all got assignments, but we can trade jobs, too. We'll have other meetings to see how our plans are working. Now I see that things can work out better when you sit down and plan together."

At your meeting, everyone in your family should be allowed to contribute to the discussion. You and your younger sisters and brothers—even the youngest—should participate. If children take part in the planning, they will be more willing to cooperate.

Your parents should lead the discussion, but they shouldn't dictate. They should respect their children's opinions and ideas.

You will need to decide what household chores have to be done, how the jobs are going to be given out, and which jobs can be modified or eliminated. Every member of your family should take part in planning household chores and suggesting which they would like to do. If someone objects strongly to an idea, the family should work out some kind of compromise. Appeal to everyone's sense of fairness. Although they may not get everything their way, everyone should at least have some say in what they will do.

Break the jobs down into daily chores, such as preparing meals; weekly chores, such as washing the kitchen floor; and those chores that only need to be done once a month or less.

Here are some topics:

- Meals: When will meals be served? Will the whole family be together at mealtime? Who will plan the meals? Who will do the cooking? Who will set the table? Who will clear the table and clean up after the meal?
- Shopping: Who will prepare the shopping list? Who will do the shopping?
- Housecleaning (dusting, vacuuming, bathrooms, kitchen floor, windows, etc.; also, home repairs, lawn maintenance): How often does each job need to be done? Who will do each job?
- Laundry: Will each person take care of their own laundry, or will one person do it all, or will everyone take turns?
- Child care: Who will take care of the younger children in the family?

Priorities

Setting priorities means arranging things in order of importance. First your family will have to agree on what is essential and what is not. State what is most important to you, personally.

If your mother is going back to work, it is especially important for her to set priorities. Your family is not going to be able to do all the household chores that they once did. And it's not necessary to do them all.

Make a list of the chores that need to be done. Number them by importance; the most essential task would be number one, and so on. To decide what is important, ask yourself, "If I do this task, how will it benefit me and my family?" Do the most important things first. Some things that are low on the list just won't get done, and that's okay.

Every family must set their own priorities and do things in their own way. Do you all work best in the morning or at night? Do you want to do things all at once, or would you rather spread chores out through the week?

The way you handle housework will differ from family to family, as it will from one person to another. Some people prefer to do a little housecleaning every day, and some want to attack it all on the weekend.

Try different ways of doing things. Keep the ones that work. Improve, change, or discard the ones that don't. Redefine your standards; is it essential to dust the bookshelves so often? Always ask: Does this task really need to be done? Must it be done the way I do it? You might be able to cut down to once a year low-priority jobs such as cleaning closets, polishing silver, or cleaning the oven.

ASSIGNING TASKS

After deciding which jobs need to be done, your family must decide who will do what job, and when. Everyone should choose the chores he or she is most comfortable with. You can exchange jobs with each other if something doesn't work out. Everyone in the family can do something to benefit the family. Every child should be given something to do, but be sure that those tasks are appropriate for the child's age and abilities.

Be flexible. Divide the chores. Let all the family members—parents and children—choose what they prefer to do. Of course, not everyone is going to get just the jobs they want and no others. But if each person gets at least one of his or her preferred jobs, the plan won't seem so bad to anyone. Jobs should be switched around from time to time so no one is doing the same task all the time. In that way, no one gets bored, and everyone learns to do every job.

Before your family meets, you can make your own list:

- chores I would like to do
- what I'm expected to do
- what others do
- chores I would like to trade with someone else

You might be surprised to find out that there is someone in your family who really wants to do the one job that no one else likes.

Everyone in the family should learn the skills needed to keep a household running smoothly. As children grow, they should learn those skills that are appropriate to their age. Household skills that the family should learn include the following:

- Cooking, and basic nutrition
- Use of kitchen appliances
- Use of hand tools
- Cleaning: dusting, vacuuming, cleaning windows and mirrors, cleaning the bathroom
- Home repairs: fixing a loose doorknob or chair leg
- Washing, ironing, mending

To Susan and Warren,
who had to cope when their mother
went back to work

Acknowledgments

I want to thank Tema Rosenblum, M.A., Family Life Educator and psychotherapist with the Jewish Family and Community Service of the Chicago Area; and her colleagues, Joan Olin, M.S., and Sheri Fox, L.C.S.W.; social workers Jane Gaitskill and Laura Pacetti; Debbie Bretag and Carol McRaith and the staff of Alternatives Youth Service Agency. All were very generous with their time and knowledge, and I appreciate it greatly.

Special thanks to the families, teens, and working parents who shared their experiences and opinions with me. The names of these family members have been changed to protect their privacy.

A B O U T   T H E   A U T H O R ◇

Gwen Packard has a Bachelor of Science in Education degree from Northwestern University and a Master of Arts in Library Science from Rosary College. Before becoming a writer, she was a children's librarian for almost fourteen years. She is a member of the Society of Children's Book Writers, the Children's Reading Round Table of Chicago, and the Off Campus Writers Workshop.

As a free-lance writer, Ms. Packard is interested in parenting issues, education, and health care. She is the author of another book for young adults, *Coping in an Interfaith Family*, which is also available from the Rosen Publishing Group.

Contents

CHAPTER 1

Why Does Mom (or Dad) Want to Go Back to Work?

So your mom is going back to work! She has not worked outside home for a long time. She has been at home every day to take care of you. That's how you have always known her. Your mom may have had a job or a career before you were born, but she has not worked in your lifetime.

There are many reasons why mothers go back to work. Sometimes it is to continue their career, whether or not there is a financial need. Sometimes they have an emotional need to be out in the world, feeling bored or lost in an empty home during the day. Very often, as it is in many families today, the main motivation is to bring home a vitally needed paycheck.

Some mothers have been on welfare for many years,

1

struggling to raise families. Child care for young children is very expensive, and the salaries from low-paying jobs would not cover the child-care and other household costs. This is one reason why mothers have to go on welfare. As their children grow and are more self-sufficient, these mothers can take part in training programs and get good jobs.

Maybe your dad is the parent going back to work. You remember when he had a job, but he's been out of work a long time. Now that he is going back to work, it's going to make a big difference in your life.

Your mom or dad may have been talking about going back to work for a long time. For that reason, it wasn't a surprise when she, or he, took the big step. On the other hand, it could have been a last-minute decision, catching you completely off guard. Either way, you, your parent, and the rest of your family will need to adjust the way you think and the way you do things at home.

Your parent may have decided to go back to work for a single reason or for a combination of them. For instance, the mother of fourteen-year-old Terry went back to work for emotional reasons and financial need. "I want recognition for my work, as well as a salary," Terry's mother says.

DIVORCE OR DEATH

It can be especially difficult for a teenager to have a parent go back to work after a divorce, or the death of a father or mother. When a parent goes back to work under these circumstances, the teenager may feel a sense of abandonment. It seems to a young person as if he or she has now lost the other parent.

Khalid Mason was thirteen and his sister Safiya was

only eight years old when their father was shot and killed in a convenience store robbery. The family had always worried about their dad. Although they knew that Mr. Mason needed to work two jobs to support his family, and that his night-time job in a convenience store was dangerous, the family was in shock when he was killed.

Khalid was very upset and missed his dad terribly. At the same time, he was worried about money. How would the family get along without his dad's income? He tried to push those thoughts out of his mind, telling himself that money was unimportant compared to the death of his father.

But Khalid found out that his mother was thinking about money, too. About a week after her husband's funeral, Mrs. Mason told her children that she would have to go back to work. She was going to take the night-time job at the convenience store.

"What?" Khalid shouted, startling his mother. He could hardly believe what he heard. "How can you go to work there? I was worried about Dad; I'll be twice as worried about you. Please don't do it, Mom."

"It will only be temporary," Mrs. Mason said. "But, if I work at night, I can be with you and Safiya during the day, and I can look for a better job. It will also give us a chance to plan how we are going to do things now that Dad is gone."

Khalid was now angry and frightened, as well as sad. But, he could see that his mother had made her decision, and she would follow through with her plans.

Sixteen-year-old Allison sensed that her parents were headed for a divorce. They had been having noisy arguments for over a year, and the arguments were getting more and more frequent. One night her dad threw a plate at her mom. No one was hurt; but her mother insisted that he move out immediately. Physical violence is totally unacceptable.

Allison had mixed feelings. She was angry, sad, and relieved at the same time. She had hoped that her parents could settle their problems peaceably. She was sad that her father was leaving. Allison loved her dad, but she was concerned about his behavior. She knew that she would miss him, even though she would see him on weekends. But Allison was also relieved that there would not be any more of those noisy arguments that seemed to be happening every night lately.

Only a few days later, Allison's mom announced that she was going back to work full time. Allison was in a state of shock. She felt as if she was being abandoned. First my dad leaves, Allison thought, and then—just at the time I need Mom the most—I find out she won't be here much either.

Allison's mother tried to explain the situation as they cleared the dinner dishes together. "I know this is hard for you, Allison. It's hard for me, too. But, it's something I have to do.

"It's ironic. Your father and I were always arguing about money. Now that we're separated, our financial situation is even worse. I have to go to work just to pay for the basic necessities. But I know that you and I can work things out so that it won't be as bad as you think."

FINANCIAL NEED

Financial need is one of the most frequent reasons a mother gives for going back to work. Even in two-parent families, both often have to work to bring in enough money for the family.

Financial need can be interpreted in different ways. Your family may need money for everyday living expenses such as food, clothing, and shelter, as well as money to put away for college or for starting a family business. Or it might mean getting a better house, taking nicer vacations, or buying luxuries.

Kate's mother wanted extra money to buy nice things for the house, to make life more pleasant—such as good lighting, or paintings. The extra income makes life easier.

Your own parents may be using the extra money to save for a college education for you and your siblings (brothers and sisters).

Mike Anderson's parents planned far into the future to pay for his college education. Mike's mother did not work outside the home until Mike was twelve. Then she went to law school on a scholarship. She had always wanted to be a lawyer; she also knew that, with a lawyer's salary, she could help pay the college tuition for Mike and his younger sister, Sara.

Financial need can be sudden and serious. If a father loses his job or his business fails, if he is disabled or dies, the mother may have to get a job even if she prefers to remain home. The whole family is upset.

REEMPLOYMENT

Parents may return to work after being unemployed or on welfare for a long time. In today's economy, many large and small businesses are laying people off, whether they are auto workers, secretaries, salespeople, or computer engineers.

If your dad is unemployed, he has probably been looking for work for a long time. For him, getting a new job and going back to work is a positive step. He may be returning to the same company that laid him off in the first place, doing the same type of work in another company, or doing completely different work than he had done before.

Your dad may be going back to work after recovering from a prolonged illness or a serious injury, like Mack's father.

When Mack Foster was fifteen, his dad injured his back in an automobile accident. He had to be in the hospital for several weeks and then at home for over two months. Mr. Foster worked for a small company. His boss was concerned about Mr. Foster's condition, and he promised to hold the job for Mack's dad until he recovered and could return to work.

Luckily, Mr. Foster had insurance to help pay for the hospitalization costs and the lost wages. Mack's mother increased her own hours of work to help pay for the family's basic needs.

At first, after Mr. Foster got out of the hospital, he and Mack were limited to friendly chats when Mack got home from school. Mack thought it was nice to have someone there. He and his dad had always gotten along well. But usually the two of them were so busy during the week and on weekends that they didn't have much time to talk about school or sports or other things that interested them.

After a while, as Mack's dad gained strength, he was able to help Mack with some of his homework. Father and son started to work together on a complex jigsaw puzzle. When his mother was working late, Mack and his dad would start dinner together. Mack grew accustomed to having his dad around, and he thought it was great.

After almost three months, Mr. Foster went back to work part time. He could still be home when Mack got home from school, so their routine continued.

- Gardening and lawn care
- Simple automotive care
- First aid

In Jay's family, his dad helps with some of the household work and with the laundry. Jay takes out the garbage every night, and his sister Claudia does the vacuuming and dusting.

In the Larson family, Mrs. Larson went back to work when Wendy and Joey were in junior high school. After that, Wendy and Joey shared many of the household chores. They took turns washing the dishes and doing all the laundry.

Planning the housework and dividing it up is important, and it can be done in an interesting, fun way. Author Irvina Siegel Lew* suggests a household management card game. List each chore on a separate 3″ × 5″ card. Divide the cards into categories such as daily chores, weekly chores, etc. Deal out the cards to each family member as if you were playing a card game. Each player accepts the cards he or she receives, or they can reject a card by trading with someone else in the family. You can play this game as often as you want to, allowing family members to alternate jobs.

Another way to divide chores is to make a chart. Every family member is assigned a specific job on a specific day. Or distribute the chores using a point system. Allot more points for the harder or less-desirable chores. Each one in the family gets assignments that add up to an equal number of points.

You could try a housework lottery. Write down each

* Irvina Siegel Lew, *You Can't Do It All; Ideas that Work for Mothers Who Work* (New York: Atheneum, 1986), p. 92.

chore on a small piece of paper and put the papers in a box, hat, or jar. Each person pulls out a slip of paper in turn until all are drawn. Whatever you draw is your assignment for the week. Chores can be traded. They can be rotated after the first week.

Post a list of all the chores and who is responsible for them. Set a time when each job must be completed and check the job off when it is finished. A check-off job list will remind everyone what their jobs are, as well as show them that they each have a share in getting the work done. They are each a part of the team.

Not every activity has to be assigned to a single person. Many chores can be shared by the family. This not only makes the effort easier; it becomes a time for the family to be together. The preparation and clean-up of dinner is one event that can be shared by the family.

If your family decide to do the housework on an all-at-once basis, you can designate one evening a week just for chores. Every family member has his assignment, and everyone works until all the jobs are completed.

You will also need to set aside time on the weekends for home repairs and housecleaning. Do short errands on weekdays and save longer errands for the weekend. You can do your grocery shopping on the weekends. If parents and teens go together, you can divide the list in half and save time. Or you can shop on your own or with friends. If you are giving a party you should get your own supplies. You know exactly what you and your friends want anyway

Negotiating

You may be so busy with school activities or your own job, that you are home even less than your parent is. This may mean that, when you are planning the household chores with your parent, you have to negotiate, or bargain, to get a better arrangement. You may be able to trade doing some chores for special privileges. For instance, if you take care of younger sisters and brothers part of the week, you get free time to be with your friends. Your special situation will have to be worked out with the rest of your family.

Sixteen-year-old Amy had to negotiate with her family. Amy was working, driving, and involved in many school activities. She had always helped around the house, with dinner or washing the dishes. However, when Amy got to high school she often didn't get home in time for dinner or to help with the dishes. When she did get home, she was usually too tired to do household chores. And, of course, she still had homework to do.

Amy's younger brother, Kurt, complained. He was doing his own chores, and he was asked to do some of Amy's chores, too. Amy's mother agreed. It wasn't fair to Kurt. Maybe Amy would have to give up some of her activities.

Amy was mortified. She couldn't give up any of her activities. So she negotiated with her parents and brother. If Kurt would do her chores during the week, Amy would do his chores on the weekend. She would also drive Kurt to his sports events on the weekend, and do some of the laundry.

Kurt still grumbled, but Amy's mother thought the idea was worth a try. It worked out fine.

FREE TIME

It's essential to build in time for relaxation and fun. It takes careful planning to make everything come into balance. We all need time for schoolwork, participation in sports and other after-school activities, leisure activities, and friends.

Plan after-school hours so you have time for recreation as well as homework and chores. But don't participate in so many activities that you are overwhelmed.

Of course, weekends are a great time for fun and social activities. This can be family time. You can make plans to be with your parents, by yourself, or with friends. If you have sports practice or a game on the weekend, encourage your family to attend. Having your family there will make you and your teammates feel good.

Be sure to set aside time for the family to do things together. If your family takes care of household responsibilities efficiently during the week, you can have more fun time together on the weekends. If you and your family get your separate chores and some homework done before dinner, then you can have fun together during and after dinner.

When a parent goes back to work, it's important for your family to talk and to plan together. Next, you have to put your plans to work. You have to get organized.

CHAPTER ◇ 4

Get Organized!

Margo Becker was having the same dream again. In her dream, she had finally reached the classroom where she would take her final exam. She had been searching for hours. As she reached for the doorknob, she heard her mother's voice in the distance.

"Margo! Margo!" Mrs. Becker yelled from the kitchen. "Get up now or you'll be late for school."

Margo rolled over in bed, opened one eye and looked at the clock. Suddenly, she was wide awake. It was really late. Why didn't her mother wake her up earlier? Margo had to give a speech in English class this morning, so she wanted to look especially nice.

Margo managed to find her slippers and staggered over to her closet. She knew exactly what she wanted to wear. She pulled out her best jeans. Oh, no! The top button was missing. Margo remembered that it had popped when she reached to swing at a high and wide fast ball the other day after school. Well, at least she got a base hit.

Why didn't Mom sew that button on for her? She always used to. Oh, yeah, Mom doesn't have time to do things like sew on buttons now that she is working full time. I was supposed to do it myself, but I forgot, Margo thought.

Margo rummaged through a messy drawer looking for her yellow sweater, but found it on the floor. If Mom would only do the dusting like she used to, there wouldn't be so much dust on my sweater, Margo thought. Well, the dust can be brushed off, but not that red stain from Saturday night's dessert.

"I guess I've got to wear something completely different." She finally found a decent pair of jeans and a sweater. Then she had to find earrings. It seemed like all the earrings she wanted to wear were missing their pairs. Should she wear unmatched earrings? It might make a fashion statement—or it might make a statement that she was a klutz.

"Margo!" her mother yelled again from the kitchen. "I'm leaving for work now. Have a good breakfast. Don't forget to take your lunch."

Margo stopped dead in her tracks. Take my lunch? she asked herself. I didn't even *make* my lunch! "Mom, wait! I need the car to go to the dentist after school." There was no response. Her mom had already left. "Oh, great! Now I have to get to the dentist by taking two buses."

As Margo tried to gather up her loose homework papers, she vowed to start planning better. "I definitely plan to write up a plan," she said out loud. "I just hope I remember!"

PLAN AHEAD

Planning will help you avoid the problems of mismanagement. You don't want to spend too much time on tasks that should take only a moment. You certainly don't want to waste time doing unnecessary tasks, like trying to find the right clothes on a busy school morning.

It's vital to plan. The night before, lay out the clothes you are going to wear, including accessories such as belts and jewelry. Then you will see ahead of time if a button is missing, a hem is loose, or a shirt needs pressing. You can sew on that button or press that shirt yourself. You can't ask Mom to do it any more.

Have a place in your home—usually the kitchen is best—where you keep the things that help the family stay organized: bulletin board, shopping list, calendar, emergency numbers, repair list, and task list. Include a timetable that shows, for example, when Mom or Dad will be working, who gets the car, who will do what, and when.

Mornings, everything the family does should be aimed at getting out of the house and starting the day off on the right foot. Everyone should have their own alarm clock. Everyone should make their own bed. You also need to plan who uses the bathroom at what time and for how long. If there is not enough hot water for every member of the family to take a shower or bath on the same morning, you will have to designate who takes one on which day.

If you have to get a hair cut or buy prom clothes, and you want your parent to drive you or be with you, she or he needs to know ahead of time.

Prepare lunches the night before and place them in the refrigerator. Put items that are to be taken to school or work—such as books, athletic equipment, and lunch bags with items that don't need refrigeration—in a specific place near the door. The lunch bag near the door will remind you to get the rest of your lunch out of the refrigerator before you leave.

In Ken's family, from seven to eight every school night,

the television is turned off. Then it's time for everyone—fourteen-year-old Ken, his two younger brothers, and even his mom—to get things ready for the next day. Book bags are prepared, clothes selected, lunches fixed.

Planning Meals

On your list of priorities, food shopping and preparing meals will be near the top. You and your family must figure out how you are going to take care of meals. It can be fun and even educational, as you keep in mind balanced meals and good nutrition. Every member of the family should be able to make suggestions. If your family is used to getting together for breakfast and dinner most of the time, you need to decide whether you want to continue that tradition after your parent goes back to work.

If you are going to eat, you need to shop for food. That's another major task that has to be taken care of. To simplify meal planning and shopping, try to shop only once a week. Post the menu plans on the kitchen bulletin board. The weekly shopping list will be based on these plans. Your mom may plan the shopping, but each one in your family should write down their individual needs on the shopping list.

Mealtime—especially dinner—is a great time for the family to work together and be together. It's not easy to get everyone together at the same time, but you can solve that problem by having the people who come home early have a snack so they can wait for a late dinner. Then the whole family can eat together after the last person gets home.

Laura's mother, a lawyer, often works twelve hours a day, but she still makes a nice family dinner three or four times a week. On those nights, the family doesn't eat until late. "I think it is critically important for a family to be together like that," Laura's mother says. On the nights Laura's mother doesn't cook, Laura or her dad makes dinner.

Some nights it may be impossible for your family to get together for dinner. Occasionally, a parent must work overtime or attend a late meeting. Often teenagers have sports, rehearsals, or a job to go to after school. Not everyone can be home for dinner every night at the regular time. In Tracey's home, it is understood that anyone who isn't home for dinner at the appointed time makes his or her own dinner.

If schedules allow, try to prepare and eat breakfast together. This can be a time when everyone reviews schedules for the day and plans when they will get together again.

You can try different methods of assigning the meal planning and cooking. The whole family could work together, or individuals could take turns fixing meals, or perhaps just the children could fix meals.

The whole family could get together once a week to cook double batches, or several meals at a time. These meals would be frozen to be reheated on busy days.

You may decide that the children in your family can do all the cooking. The teenagers can supervise their younger sisters and brothers. In the Gonzalez family, each child who is old enough is assigned a whole week to make dinner. They discuss menus with their mother and plan the shopping with her. Everyone in the family has learned to cook, and everyone enjoys it.

Before she went back to work, Mrs. Quinn always made brown-bag lunches for her husband and her two children, Ross and Nina. After she started working full time, Mrs.

Quinn not only expected Ross and Nina to make their own lunches, but she also asked them to make lunch for her and for their father.

Some mothers like to continue making lunches for the family, even after they have gone back to work. Paul and Diana's mother still makes their lunches.

"Mom's funny," Paul says. "She thinks making lunch is a way to connect with us during the day. Sometimes she puts a note or some extra cookies in my lunch bag."

If you do fix your own lunch to take with you to school, try to make it in the evening before you go to bed. Mornings are usually too hectic for lunch-making.

Laundry

There are many ways you can attack the laundry. Your family should consider the choices together. You can decide to do the laundry once a week or every day. If you take things to the local Laundromat, you can do many loads at once.

Everyone can do their own clothes, or one person can do all the wash for one week. Everyone else in the family then brings what they want washed to the person who is designated to do the wash that week.

To organize the laundry, you might provide everyone in the family with his or her own hamper. Or have a big hamper that everyone uses. It's also a good idea to consider using three or four hampers, so you can separate the different types of laundry. For example, dark colors can all go in one hamper, delicate or thin fabrics in another, and soiled work clothes and sports clothes in another. Only what is in the hamper gets washed. Once a week, each family member can remove the sheets from his or her bed and throw the sheets into the washer.

Help stamp out ironing! Whether you do laundry at home or at a Laundromat, take wash-and-wear items out of the dryer promptly so they won't wrinkle. Sort clothes right at the dryer and fold them. Take hangers to the dryer and hang the clothes up as soon as you take them out.

Whether you are doing your own personal laundry, or taking care of other people's, you need to be careful. Read the labels sewn into the garments to see the washing instructions.

Take the time to educate yourselves about fabrics— knits and wovens, and wools, cottons, synthetics, and blends.

Tom, fifteen, his fourteen-year-old sister Nicole, and younger brother David take turns doing the family laundry. Each one is assigned a week at a time. One week Tom got careless and washed his sister's clothes in hot water. When he pulled Nicole's knit shirt out of the machine, it would fit a three-year-old.

Nicole screamed, "Tom ruined my favorite shirt! What am I going to do?"

"I'm really sorry," Tom said, and he meant it. "I must have pushed the hot water button instead of the medium button by mistake."

Nicole, Tom, and their mother discussed the problem. "There's nothing we can do about the shirt," their mother said.

Tom offered to save his allowance and buy Nicole a new shirt. Nicole thought that would create a hardship for Tom, so she said it wasn't necessary, but she asked him to take special care in the future. Tom agreed, saying he would go to the library and do some research on fabrics.

Child Care

If you have brothers and sisters who are too young to stay home by themselves, you and your parents must discuss how they will be cared for. You will have to work together to decide who will be responsible for the child care after school and in the evening. You need to take into account your parents' schedules and your own: how much time you spend at school or work, how much time you need for homework, sports, meetings, and other activities.

You may be asked to take care of your younger sisters and brothers occasionally or on a regular basis, especially when your parents are working. Ask your parent to post a schedule, so you will know when it's your turn to baby-sit. Give your parent a copy of your schedule, so she will know when you are available. You should discuss with your parents specific rules about time for watching television or doing homework, meal preparation, and other chores. You and the younger children should understand these rules and follow them.

Discuss with your parent the idea of enrolling the younger children in an after-school program. These programs provide many benefits for a child. Children can be together with others their own age and take part in a variety of physical and creative activities. Information on after-school programs is given in Chapter 10.

Because Ruthie drives to high school every day, her mother sometimes asks her to pick up her younger brother Russell at school and take him home or to his own activities. If her mother has a late meeting, either work-

related or not, Ruthie stays home to watch Russell. But
Ruthie is always told in advance when she's needed for
child care, so she can adjust her plans. She knows she will
be asked in advance, so she is never surprised.

If you have after-school activities or a job, you won't be
able to care for younger brothers and sisters every day.
Your parent might be able to arrange with a friend or
relative to take of them.

Antoine's great-grandmother Ella lives near Antoine's
city apartment. Antoine has a job, so every day after school
his sister Ayisha goes to Great-grandmother's apartment
and stays until around supper time. Ayisha likes going
there. She has a snack, does her homework. And, because
Great-grandmother cares for other children in the
neighborhood, Ayisha usually has some one to play with.

Antoine picks Ayisha up when he's finished with work.
Sometimes he just rings the bell. Often Great-
grandmother calls down, "Come up here and say hello to
me." Antoine enjoys these visits. He loves his great-
grandmother and thinks she's a lot of fun.

ALTERNATIVES TO HOUSEWORK

In order to have time for fun, you have to be organized
and efficient, and you have to plan. You should try to
eliminate, reduce, or modify some of the chores you used
to do. Do fewer tasks in less time or in a different way.

You should also consider some alternatives to doing
housework and other tasks. For instance, to avoid time-
consuming shopping trips, you can use catalogs and order
over the phone. Be aware, though, that you will pay more
for things bought this way. Use the shopping services
offered by some stores; special sales people can make your

selection for you and have it delivered. Use an answering machine to leave messages for each other.

Some alternatives to doing housework may cost money, so your family needs to give them consideration and decide whether they are worth the extra cost. Those alternatives include having a house-cleaning service or a lawn service, and ordering groceries or other items from a store that delivers.

BE FAIR AND SHARE

As you plan the household tasks and assign them to family members, try to be fair to everyone in the family. Even the youngest child has a sense of fairness. Don't ask one person—parent or child—to be accountable for too many jobs. Family members of almost any age can be given some kind of household responsibility. Just be sure that the work given to a child is appropriate for that child's age.

Don't assign tasks according to gender, or based on stereotypes: "This is woman's work." "A man can do this better." Sometimes teenage daughters are expected to do more work than their fathers and brothers. Be aware of that when you're planning. Ask yourself: Are the boys being given more freedom? Are the girls being given more responsibility? Or the other way around?

Everyone, male and female, should learn how to use stoves safely, do the laundry, and perform simple home repairs, according to author Earl Grollman. Girls should know how to mow the lawn, and boys should know how to use a sewing machine. Both can take care of younger children. No one person, not even your mom or dad, is the *only* one who can do a particular task.

Even though the teenagers in the family are capable

of taking on a lot of responsibility, they should not be expected to do more than their fair share of the work. Because of school activities and their own work schedule, teenagers may be home even fewer hours than their parents.

Your parent should be fair to you, and you should be fair to your parent, too. In many families, the mother still does most of the housework, even if she is working full time. A mother who works outside the home should insist that her family share the chores, and the family should be ready and willing to share. It's a team effort.

THE FAMILY TEAM

No matter what kind of a family you come from—whether there's a single parent or two parents, lots of kids or just you—your family can and should operate as a team.

The family team is like a well-run sports team. Everyone contributes; everyone has a part to play. Every team has a common goal, whether it's the high school basketball team trying to win the state championship or the home team getting all the household chores done on time. Mom may have to do some convincing about the importance of the home team goals. You might say she becomes the coach.

Home belongs to everyone who lives in it. Its upkeep is everyone's obligation. Everyone in the family—including teens and younger children—should be interested in the maintenance of the home. Don't think of it as helping your mother with *her* chores, even if your mother was the only one who did these things before she went back to work.

If your family looks upon doing housework as *helping* rather than sharing, you won't have your hearts in it.

How do mothers convince their families that they should be part of the team? Abbie's mom is very matter of fact. She shrugs her shoulders and asks, "What did I do to convince my family to do housework? It had to be done, and that's that."

For Greg and Nick's mom, it wasn't so easy. "With my family, I had to force everyone to cooperate," she says. "It's not surprising there was a problem getting everyone to contribute. Dad and the kids got spoiled because I have been doing all the housework for as long as they can remember."

STANDARDS

As players on a team, each family member has assigned tasks. Each one is responsible for doing the job correctly and on time; that means planning the work, getting supplies, remembering to do it, and then doing it right. Everyone should be clear on the right way to do a particular task and what will happen if the job is not done right.

Your family should all agree on the minimum standards for a job. Then you are on your own to do your work in your own way. It is up to you to plan your work and remember to do it. You should judge yourself on the quality of the job you have done.

Family members should do tasks in their own way. You can learn from your mistakes. Don't apologize for someone else's mistakes.

Once the group has assigned all the tasks, each person should be concerned only about his or her job. Other family members should live with or ignore undone chores until the person responsible does them. Parents should resist the temptation to do someone else's work because it was done wrong or not at all.

A parent should not cover for another family member's undone chores. If a person does not do a job, or does it poorly, that person should suffer the consequences. For instance, if you forget to make your lunch, you just won't have a lunch when you get to school.

Doing a good job includes doing the job at the right time. The family should plan together not only who does what chore, but when it should be done. Once your family's plan for doing the housework is established and you have written a schedule, chores must be done at the right time. You can't put off doing certain things just because you don't want to do them.

Standards should be high but reasonable. Asking a teen or younger child to do too much can create stress. Many kids don't work well under pressure. Pressuring them with too much work or too high standards may only upset them and make it less likely that they will want to cooperate.

Once your family starts working as a team, it can become a positive experience for everyone. You will have a feeling of importance and a sense of accomplishment. You will be learning new skills. And you will have the good feeling of being part of the family team.

On Your Own

Recent news stories and popular movies have depicted children staying home alone. The fact is, millions of grade school children—and millions more teenagers—are home alone at least part of every day.

Before your mom or dad went back to work, your parent may have been home when you were there. Coming home to an empty house or apartment will be a big change for you. This can be a negative aspect of your parent's working, or it can be a positive time. It all depends on planning.

With your parents, you need to establish some rules for the time that you are home alone. You should discuss what activities you will take part in, what safety and security measures you should take, how to handle emergencies, and how you should take care of younger sisters and brothers, if that is part of your duties.

You should also discuss your feelings about staying home alone. Some teenagers like the idea of being responsible for themselves and being independent; others feel lonely or even abandoned when left alone.

Be sure to let your parent know if you are nervous

about staying home alone. Your parent should know if you are anxious about being lonely or fearful for your safety. Don't hesitate to talk about these feelings with your parent because you're afraid that she or he might think you're a "baby" or might be annoyed with you. Adults have the same concerns. By discussing these worries together, you and your parents can plan safety measures and activities that will help to ease your anxieties. Parents should never assume that their children know about safety.

SETTING RULES

You are confident that you can take care of yourself and that you can handle responsibility. Your parents trust you. But you still need some rules, some guidelines.

Children and teenagers who spend time alone can learn responsibility. They also need to have a feeling of security. Setting up rules can teach responsibility as well as establish a feeling of security. Discuss with your parents what rules they want you to follow when you are taking care of yourself. Consider the reason for each one. If you do not agree with some of the guidelines, tell your parents your reasons. Perhaps you can negotiate or compromise on some of them.

Reasonable rules, along with a feeling of responsibility and security, can help you to say no to unacceptable behavior such as drinking and drug abuse.

If you are responsible for your younger brothers and sisters when an adult is not home, there are a few questions you should go over with your parents.

- What are you expected to do for your sisters and brothers?

- What are they expected to do?
- Must they obey you?
- How are you supposed to resolve conflicts that might develop?
- What activities are the younger children allowed to engage in?
- How much time are they allowed for television or video games?
- Are they allowed to leave the house? If so, where can they go?
- What kind of snacks can they have?

Write down the answers to these questions and, along with the other rules, post them on the household bulletin board.

KEEP IN TOUCH

The rules your parent wants you to follow will be influenced by her ideas about discipline and responsibility, and how much responsibility she thinks you are ready to handle. For instance, you may be allowed to have friends in your home when your parent is not there, or you may not.

Teenagers Kevin and Shawna are allowed to have friends over if their mother knows about it in advance. If they go to a friend's house, they have to tell their mother. "I know Mom trusts us," Kevin says. "But she needs to know where we are, and our friend's address and phone number, so she can reach us in an emergency."

Even though you are a teenager, and you consider yourself independent, your parent or another adult should know where you are after school. If you are at home, check in by phone. If you go to a friend's home or other location, let your parents know, unless you have informed them in advance where you will be. Your parents may want you to phone one of them or leave a note or message if you leave the house.

Jamila, who lives in the city, has to call her mother twice when she goes someplace other than her home. "Mom gets so worried, I have to call her before I leave to tell her where I'm going," Jamila says. "Then I have to call her again to tell her I got there safely."

Use the phone to communicate during the day. You can phone a parent—or another adult if a parent cannot be reached—to say you are home. You should have someone to call besides your parents in case of emergency or when you are worried about your safety.

Have a phone list of emergency numbers and keep it posted near every telephone in your home. Your list of emergency phone numbers should include the following:

- Mom's full name, workplace, and work phone
- Dad's full name, workplace and work phone
- Neighbors
- Relatives
- Doctors, offices and home phone numbers
- Fire Department (also 911, if available)
- Police Department (also 911, if available)
- Ambulance (also 911, if available)
- Hospital
- Poison control center
- Building superintendent (if you live in an apartment building)
- Gas company, plumber, furnace repair (if you live in a house)
- Your home address and phone number

Everyone in your family should know about dialing 911—or 0, where 911 is not available—in case of emergency. You should discuss ahead of time what an emergency is, so everyone can act quickly if one occurs. When you call an emergency number such as 911, it is important not to hang up until told to do so.

You should memorize certain phone numbers, such as your parents' work phones. Know the names and phone numbers of at least two neighbors that you can call in an emergency. Always have enough change on hand to use a pay phone.

Each member of the family should have his or her own key. Never lend your key to a friend or stranger. Don't hide a key near your house; someone may find out about it. Keep an extra key in the home of a neighbor that you trust. Work out a plan of what to do in case your key is lost or if you are locked out of the house.

SAFETY MEASURES

When you come home to an empty house, there are safety pointers you need to follow to protect yourself and the household. Do not open the door to strangers. Don't let anyone know there is no adult at home. Don't give information over the phone. Don't tell anyone the exact hours your parent works, or that your family is going away on a trip. Use an answering machine to screen calls.

Thirteen-year-old Nell explains some of her family's phone rules: "When my parents aren't home, I answer the phone by saying, 'Mom is busy and can't come to the phone right now. If you leave a message, I'll have her call you right back.' I don't even answer the doorbell."

Never enter a house or apartment that looks as if it has been broken into. Be cautious if you see a broken window or an open door, or if you observe a suspicious person. Go to a neighbor or near-by pay phone and call your parent or the police. You should be able to sense danger and avoid it. Trust your own judgment.

Fourteen-year-old Ryan was laughing as he and his friends got off the school bus late on a Friday afternoon. But Ryan's smile quickly turned to a frown as he approached his house. Even though it was getting dark, Ryan could see that the window near the back door was broken and the door was part way open.

Ryan was frightened and angry. But he knew what to do because he had discussed with his parents how to handle this type of situation. Ryan did not go into his house, but went to a neighbor's that he knew would be home.

From the neighbor's house, Ryan called the police. He also phoned his mother at work. "I'll come right home," his mother said.

In the meantime, the police came. They searched Ryan's house and found no one there. It looked as if the intruders had not taken anything either. "Maybe they heard me laughing with my friends and ran away," Ryan said.

By the time Ryan's mother got home, the police were writing up their report. "I'm really proud of you," Ryan's mother told him. "You took care of the problem."

Ryan felt good. "I'm glad we talked about how to handle an emergency situation," he said. "Even though I was scared, I also felt that I was doing the right thing."

If you are going to be home alone, you will want to feel safe and secure. You want to do what you can to avoid personal injury. You also want to discourage home intruders. Check your home and set up a safe home environment. A member of your local police or fire department may come out and make a safety check of your house.

Have an alarm system in your home. Install locks on doors and windows, and see that they are kept locked. Be sure your home is equipped with smoke detectors and a fire extinguisher. If your family owns a gun, keep it unloaded and locked up.

If you live in a city apartment, you need to take special precautions. If your apartment is on the first or second floor, install iron bars on all the windows; in any apartment, put bars on the windows in or near exit doors. Be sure that window bars can be easily opened from the inside in case of fire.

Look around the house and remove or repair potential causes of accidents, such as loose or frayed electrical wires, slippery scatter rugs, unstable book cases, and poisonous cleaning supplies. The following are some items to have on your home safety check list. You can get even more detailed information from your local library or organizations such as the National Safety Council. See Chapter 10 for a list of organizations.

- Be sure electrical appliances, including lamps and cords, are in good condition.
- Carpeting and rugs should not be torn or slippery.
- Keep curtains away from the stove.
- Hazardous materials should be kept out of the reach of young children.
- Use pot holders.
- Know how to use the microwave oven and other appliances.
- Unplug appliances when not in use.
- Use a stepladder, not a chair, to get hard-to-reach items.
- Use night lights in hallways and near stairs.
- Put a non-skid mat in the bathtub.

- Keep electrical appliances away from tub or shower.
- Keep flashlights near all beds.

Everyone in the family who is going to use the stove should know about its proper use and safety precautions. Do not wear loose clothing, especially with long sleeves, while working at the stove; tie back your hair; keep paper and cloth items away from the stove; keep pot handles turned away from the front. Whoever is the last to leave the house in the morning should check that all appliances—such as the toaster, stove, and oven—are turned off.

Learn to handle firearms safely, whether your family owns a gun or not. If you do have firearms in the house, be sure they are kept unloaded and locked up, with ammunition locked up in a separate location. Children and teens should know about firearm safety, but they should not have access to guns and other firearms.

A partial list of some of the safety equipment recommended for your home by the National Safety Council*:

- Flashlights; keep several around the house, and be sure batteries are functioning
- Smoke detectors: check the batteries regularly
- All-purpose fire extinguishers; everyone in the family should know how to use them properly
- A well-stocked first aid kit; all family members should know basic first aid, and should know the purpose of each of the items in the kit
- A step stool or utility ladder

* Carole Huybrecht and Mary Cullen (eds.), "Take Safety Home with the Right Equipment," *Volunteers' Voice For Community Safety & Health*, July/Aug., 1990, p. 1:

- Non-slip mats or decals in bathtubs and shower stalls
- Safety goggles and gloves for cleaning and yard work
- Pot holders and oven mitts
- Safe storage areas for kitchen utensils and equipment such as knives and appliances

There should be at least two first aid kits in your home, one in the kitchen and one in the bathroom. If you live in a house with more than one level, have a first aid kit on each level. You should know how to treat minor cuts and burns. The number for the Poison Control Center should be on the emergency phone number list.

Rehearse special situations so you know what to do in an emergency. Cover all the "what if's." You should know how to respond to an emergency, whether it is an injury that needs immediate care, a gas leak, or a fire. Have an emergency evacuation plan. Practice it and include all members of the family.

In case of a fire, take the following precautions:

- Leave your house or apartment immediately, lead younger children out, do not stop to take anything else with you.
- If you live in an elevator apartment building, do not use the elevator; use the stairs.
- Call the fire department from a neighbor's house.

Your family should also discuss what to do when there is a power failure in the house, or when there is a severe weather warning such as a tornado or severe thunder storm.

With your parents, go over the rules of recreational

safety, such as appropriate behavior near water: the ocean, lakes, rivers, or pools. Stay away from dangerous areas such as railroad tracks or construction sites.

You might feel more secure at home if you own a pet, especially a dog. A dog may scare away intruders and give you a feeling of reassurance. Dogs and other pets provide companionship and help develop responsibility, too.

FREEDOM AND RESPONSIBILITY

When your parent goes back to work and you are on your own, you will have a new sense of freedom. With your increased independence, you may be tempted to risk doing something against the law such as getting involved with drugs or alcohol. You need to balance your new freedom and independence with a sense of responsibility.

You know when you are doing things that will get you in trouble with the law and with your parent. Before you act, you should think about the consequences of your actions. Ask yourself, What will happen to me if I do this? How will it affect me, my parent, and others? (And don't think that you won't get caught!)

You should also ask yourself *why* you are doing things you should not be doing. Is it because of anger toward your parent? Or because you have nothing better to do with your time? You may need to talk to a school counselor to work out your feelings of anger. A school counselor can also help you find positive after-school activities such as clubs and other youth service organizations. (See Chapter 10 for more suggestions.)

Don't let your friends pressure you. Don't be afraid of being called a baby or a chicken when you *don't* want to go along with antisocial behavior. Stay away from kids who are liable to get in trouble. If you are with someone who commits a crime, you can be arrested, too.

Get involved with sports, clubs, volunteering in a day care center or a political organization. With planning, you can also enjoy a variety of activities when you're at home alone.

KEEPING BUSY AT HOME

If you are involved with sports or clubs after school, you may not be home alone very often. In fact, some days your parent may get home before you do. If you don't have activities before or after school, you may be by yourself part of every day. Either way, you should plan how you will spend your time when you are by yourself. Some things to consider include exercising, reading, doing creative projects like painting or drawing, doing homework, or listening to music.

Robert is thirteen years old. After school, a few of Robert's friends like to run in and out of neighborhood stores, acting michievously. A couple of times his friends John and Bernard have been taken in to the police station.

Robert was worried that if he stayed with these friends, he would get into trouble, too. So he decided to go home after school even though he would be alone for several hours.

At first, when Robert headed straight for home, his friends teased him. "Mama's baby," John called him. But, after a while, when Robert didn't change his mind, they just let him go.

When he gets home, Robert has a snack and does his homework. Then he works on a complicated model ship. "When I'm alone is the best time to work on my ship model," Robert says. "It takes a lot of concentration, and there's no one around to bother me." He watches some television, and then does something to get dinner started.

It all takes good planning. Robert and his mother plan together what Robert will have to eat when he gets home, as well as what they will have for dinner and what he can do to help start the dinner. "We usually make plans after dinner on Friday. Then I buy the food on Saturday morning, because Mom has to work on Saturdays, too," Robert says.

At home after school, you have the opportunity to do creative projects. If you like to do handicrafts such as model-building, if you like to paint pictures or play a musical instrument, this is a great time to do it. Some of the tasks you don't usually consider fun can be done creatively for fun when you're home alone. You can cook for fun. Experiment with new dishes, or show off your cooking skills by creating a fabulous dessert for the family. You can also read for fun; catch up on the latest best seller.

Exercising is an interesting pursuit that you can do by yourself. It's good for you, too. You can exercise outdoors by running, walking, or bike riding. You can play soccer or shoot baskets with a group. You can exercise indoors, too. Find ideas on making your own inexpensive exercise equipment, at the library.

Another good way to spend your time alone is to do your homework or help a younger sister or brother with his homework. You can do your assigned household chores, start dinner, set the table, or clean your room. And what about that loose button or spot on your shirt that you meant to take care of?

When you are talking about rules, discuss with your parents the amount of time they think you should be allowed for watching television and which shows you should watch.

If your parents leave for work before you leave for school in the morning, you need to think about how to fill that time in, too. You may be able to join a before-school sports program, if there is one at your school or community center.

If you do not like the idea of being home alone after school, if you feel lonely or bored, you can try to find an after-school program through your church, scouts, library, community center, or school. You may be able to assist in after-school programs for younger children whose parents are working.

A young teen can go to a sitter's home after school. You should feel comfortable and safe with the sitter. Be sure to tell your parent if the sitter is not acting appropriately. If you prefer to be with friends, you should be able to go to your friends' homes occasionally, or have them over to your house. You need to work this out with your parents and set up some guidelines.

During extended school vacations, such as winter break or summer vacation, being on your own can present a problem. Plan well ahead with your family how each child will spend the time. Younger children may be able to go to day camp at the YMCA or community center. You may be able to work at a local business. Or you can start your own business mowing lawns or shoveling snow, baby sitting, or helping in the homes of other working mothers.

Of course, it would be great if your mom and dad could get some time off from work at the same time as your school break. Then the whole family could do something together. However, this may not be possible, especially if your parent has just started a new job.

SICK AT HOME

In addition to after-school and vacation periods, you may also find yourself alone when you are sick. Your family should set a policy deciding under what conditions you or your sisters and brothers will stay home without an adult when you are sick. Teens can take care of themselves when they have a cough or cold. But no one should go to school with a serious illness.

Because every illness can be different in its degree of seriousness and how it affects the sick person, each case has to be judged on its own merits. It is up to your parent to decide whether a child can be left alone or if the parent or another caregiver should be there.

The decision to leave a sick child alone may also depend on whether the parents can use sick leave—time they are given for their own illness—to care for a child at home. If they cannot take a whole day off, they might arrange to be home at least part of the day. In some areas a service is available in which a hospital sends someone to take care of a sick child. This can be expensive. When a child is home ill, the parent should phone several times a day, whether there is a caregiver there or the child is alone.

"If I stayed home because I was sick, I was able to take care of myself. I just slept," fifteen-year-old Cathy says. "If my younger brother John was sick, Mom stayed home, or she asked a relative or friend to be there. Her job allowed sick days, and she used them to take care of him. John was never expected to stay alone if he was ill. But he never stayed home unless he had a high fever or a stomach flu."

Teenagers Marty and Anita stay home by themselves when they are sick. "Even when we were younger, we would stay home with a lot of fruit juice, the TV remote, and the telephone," Marty says. "My parents don't stay home. Mom says she doesn't like to hover over us. If we have a medical emergency or an accident, there are people we can call, like our grandparents."

GETTING AROUND

When your parent goes back to work and you're on your own, transportation may become a problem. How do you get to and from school and your activities? You may have to walk or bike places, take public transportation, rely on someone else to drive, or curtail your activities because you don't have wheels.

Patrick was lucky. When he was in the eighth and ninth grades, his older sister, Frannie, drove him where he needed to go. Now that Frannie is in college, Patrick's friends drive him, and he will soon he able to drive himself.

If you can drive, but your parents hesitate to let you use the car, you might try negotiating. For instance, you can offer to help out on the weekends with errands or shopping if they let you use the car for your needs. You can also offer to drive the younger children to their activities.

Occasionally, parents' work schedules allow them to drive their children places. Gary's father, who is finished with work by three in the afternoon, drives Gary to friends' homes, to the store for school supplies, and to the library.

Most teens don't have access to a car. Ed has to take his bike when he wants to go someplace. "Because my mom is always worried about me riding in traffic, I have to call her when I get where I'm going," Ed says. If a bike is your transportation, review bike safety rules. The following is a summary of bike rules. You can get a detailed list at your local police department or state safety office.

- Wear a helmet.
- Check the condition of your bike: front light; reflectors on front and back and on wheels and pedals; gears, handlebars, seat, and accessories.
- Ride single file, one to a bike.
- Ride close to the right edge of the road, except in the city, where you should ride a car-door's width from parked cars.
- Watch for road hazards; avoid sewer grates and manhole covers.
- Learn the meaning of all traffic signs and signals and obey them.
- Learn arm turn signals and use them.
- Obey all traffic laws.

Take care of your bike, too.

- Register your bike with police.
- When you're at home, keep your bike out of sight, preferably inside your house or apartment.
- When you are away from home, keep your bike in sight, but locked.
- Always lock your bike!

When walking or riding a bike in city streets, always try to go with a friend. Don't take shortcuts down dark side streets or alleys. Avoid being out alone at night. Report a mugger immediately. Whatever form of transportation you use, do not hitch-hike.

Be creative in your search for transportation. You might be able to hire a driver, such as a retired or unemployed person or a college student. Perhaps a grandparent or other relative or friend can take you places, and a parent can pick you up on the way home from work. You can car-pool with friends. You might need to take a taxi in an emergency; set some money aside for just that purpose. If you cannot find transportation, you might have to select activities within walking distance.

You're fortunate if you have good public transportation in your city or town. You can get a safety tip booklet from your local transit company. Here are a few tips to start with:

- When you're using public transportation, try to go with a friend.
- Be alert; know your route and have your fare ready when boarding.
- Do not carry your wallet in your back pocket; if you carry a backpack or purse, keep it closed and hold it in front of you while riding.
- Keep valuables, such as jewelry, out of sight.
- While waiting for the subway train, stay within view or calling distance of the ticket booth.
- In the subway, sit in the car with the motorman or conductor; in a bus, sit near the driver.
- Don't cheat on your fare or allow friends to use your pass; don't smoke, litter, play loud radios, or deface property with graffiti; don't sprawl on the seat.

By following safety tips when riding on public transportation, checking for safety and security measures in your home, and being responsible for yourself when you're on your own, you are establishing positive lifestyle habits that will stay with you.

CHAPTER 6

Why Is Everyone So Emotional?

Fifteen-year-old Jórge just couldn't figure his mother out. Two weeks ago, when she went back to work as an accountant, she seemed so happy. She loved her work, and she thought she would do a good job. Jórge and his mom and dad had a family meeting and decided how the housework and the cooking would be shared. They even discussed doing things together on weekends. It's okay, Jórge thought then. Mom is going back to work, and it's not such a bad idea.

But that was two weeks ago. Today, Jórge wasn't so sure about his mom's working. It's not such a great idea after all, he thought.

Now Jórge's mom seemed angry about everything. She looked tired and confused. She seemed to be unhappy and even fearful. Even though Jórge thought that he and his dad were helping out a lot around the house, his mother yelled at him for not helping.

Jórge wasn't too happy about things himself. He felt

that he hardly ever saw his parents any more. He had to do so many things around the house that his mom used to do, it was cramping his social life. His dad was yelling at him more for no good reason, too. Why is everyone so emotional? Jórge wondered. How can people go from good moods to bad so quickly?

When a parent goes back to work, it seems as if everyone in the family is on edge. This is a big change for the whole family, not just the parent. There is added stress in the lives of all family members. This can lead to strong emotions, both positive and negative.

Your parent is going to have new emotions, too. Her feelings of pressure, fear, guilt, and depression—as well as happiness and enthusiasm—will affect your life as well as hers. She may bring home the emotions she experiences at work, such as frustration and anger.

You probably have some pretty strong emotions, too. You may be worried that things won't get done around the house as they used to. You may be angry because you don't see your parents as often now, and you may even have to compete for your parents' attention. You might feel sad or lonely, or even abandoned, because you spend a lot more time by yourself. You may be concerned about your own safety and that of your parent, too, especially if she is working in a dangerous area or at night. The situation is stressful because you have to deal with your parent's emotions as well as your own.

Your age has an effect on your attitude. If you are an older teen who has been pretty independent for several years, the changes are not going to seem as big for you or your parent. There will be less tension.

On the other hand, if you are in junior high school, or you are just entering high school and trying to establish an identity there, your situation may seem more unsure.

You are adjusting to life as a teenager as well as getting used to your parent's going back to work.

"It is harder for a teen whose mother goes back to work," says Tema Rosenblum, Family Life Educator with the Jewish Family and Community Service of Chicago. "The teenager is now going through *two* adjustments, *two* new stages."

There are many reasons for negative feelings. If you have to be home by yourself a lot, you may experience loneliness, fear for your own safety as well as your parent's, or even rejection. You might be thinking, "If my parents loved me, they'd spend more time with me."

But there are also ways of coping with these negative feelings to reduce them or eliminate them altogether. Coping with such emotions requires discussion, planning, and cooperation among all your family members. To reduce feelings of loneliness, set aside time for you and your parents to be together in the evening or on weekends. Discuss safety measures that can be taken to make you feel more secure at home. Discuss and practice emergency plans.

MIXED EMOTIONS

When your parent—whether it's your mom or dad—goes back to work, it is a time of mixed emotions for everyone. Say it's your mother. She will be happy to have found a good job; her self-esteem will increase. But she might also be fearful that she won't be able to do the job and take care of her family obligations, too. She asks herself, was it the right decision? Will I be able to do the job? Will I be able to handle the busy schedule? Am I doing the right thing for my children? Fear and anxiety can lead to anger, tension, and stress.

Sixteen-year-old Charles knew that his mother had mixed emotions when she got the opportunity to get off welfare and go to work. She wanted to work because it would bring in a lot more income, and it would make her feel much better about herself. But, at the same time, she was worried about Charles. If she was working, she wouldn't know what Charles was doing. She was afraid that he might get into trouble.

Charles wanted his mother to go to work, too. He knew it was the right thing for her to do, and he and his mother talked it over. They planned how he would spend his time after school, some days going home to do homework, other days working at a part-time job. Occasionally, Charles would go to his mother's workplace and do his homework or help out by doing errands.

You have mixed feelings about your parent's work, too. Now you can be more independent. But you might not feel very independent if you have to be home to do chores or take care of younger children instead of being out with friends or working at your own job.

You might be afraid that your needs will be lost in the shuffle. Things are being done differently than they were before, which may give you a feeling of insecurity. You may even feel a bit envious of your parent's going to work and envious of the people she is working with. They are getting her attention now.

Thirteen-year-old Rosita never admitted to her mother —or herself—that she felt envious. Her mother went back to work as a math teacher in a junior high school in another suburb. Now Rosita's mother was spending more time with eighty other thirteen-year-olds than she was spending with Rosita. Who wouldn't be jealous?

If your dad is going back to work after not working for a long time because of unemployment or sickness or injury, he is going to have mixed feelings. He is probably very happy that he found a job after looking for a long time. Or he's glad to know that he has recovered enough from his illness or injury to go back to work. Going back to work boosts his self-esteem, and it is a relief to him, too.

However, your dad may also be worried about doing a good job. If it is a new job, will he be successful? If he has not worked at his old job for a long time, will he still be able to do the work right? Will he have to catch up to those employees who have been working when he wasn't?

If your mom is the parent going back to work, your dad is still going to have a variety of emotions. Your dad may feel that your mom's job threatens his self-esteem.

On the other hand, the extra income your mother brings in reduces the pressure on your dad to be the only provider for the family. It also gives him more freedom to get a different job or go back to school part time.

DEALING WITH ANGER

When your parent goes back to work, you might react with anger. You may feel that your parent is being selfish and not thinking about your welfare. You may feel that your parents messed up their own lives by getting a divorce.

Tess was angry with both her parents for getting a divorce. Her dad wasn't keeping up with child support payments, and Tess' mother had to go to work. "It's not my fault you got divorced," Tess told her mother. "I didn't want you to get divorced. But now I'm the one who has to suffer. There's less money to spend, but I have to do more around the house. I never see my dad any more, and I hardly ever get to see you. That really makes me mad."

Fourteen-year-old Winston also reacted with anger. After his mother, a single parent, went back to work, Winston hardly ever saw her. When she came home at night, she was too tired to do anything with Winston. He started to think, "Well, maybe I won't come home either. I'll just hang out with my friends."

Luckily, Winston told his mother how angry he felt. They decided to set aside one day a week to be together. They also agreed that if Winston would help with the cooking and housecleaning, his mother wouldn't feel so tired, and they could do more things together.

In some families, feelings of anger become too serious to be resolved through discussion alone. Anger may lead to physical violence or even illness. In these cases, the family needs a counselor to help them settle differences.

DEALING WITH STRESS

There are many different sources of stress when a parent goes back to work, for the parent and her family. If a mother is afraid she will be criticized by her family or outsiders for choosing to go back to work, she may hesitate to ask others for help. This will increase the pressure she feels trying to work and take care of her other obligations at the same time.

Your dad's attitude toward your mother's working will have an effect on the family's emotions. Family tension will be much greater if your father is not happy about the idea of your mother's going back to work in the first place, than if he is supportive of the situation.

Sixteen-year-old Anna could feel the increased tension between her mom and dad after her mother went back to work. They fought more than ever, and Anna was even worried they might get a divorce.

If your parents are divorced, conflicts may seem to get worse when a parent goes back to work. Sylvie's parents were fighting so much before they separated that she was actually relieved when they decided to get a divorce. But their problems didn't end there. After the divorce, Sylvie's dad did not keep up with child-support payments. Sylvie's mother had to go to work, and now she was angrier than ever. This added to the tension she felt trying to work and take care of Sylvie and her younger brother.

Whatever causes stress for a parent can cause stress for the whole family. Because Lenny's mom had so many things to do in the morning, including taking Lenny's little brother Mitch to day care, she was always afraid she would be late to work. Then she was worried that she wouldn't be able to pick Mitch up on time. When Lenny's mom got home in the evening, she was exhausted, and she would start yelling at Lenny for no good reason. Then Mitch would start crying. It was a very stressful situation that needed resolving.

A parent's going back to work may not be the direct cause of tension in the family. However, it might intensify another emotional problem that already exists. That's the way it was in Karen's home. "My mom was always emotional, even before she began working," Karen says. "The hardest time for her was probably when my older brother left for college. That's when she went back to work, and that's when the tension level at home increased. But it didn't increase because Mom worked. It went up because the family went through a lot of changes outside of Mom's job."

Even in a family that is supportive, there can be stress. In sixteen-year-old Sam's family, everyone is supportive of his mother's working. "But there is still a lot of pressure on our family. Probably because we're all so busy. We all feel like we're doing twenty things at once," Sam says.

Don't be surprised if your working parents seem to be "stressed out." They often feel overwhelmed, as if they were doing too many things at once. They want to meet high standards at work and still be good parents. They try to keep everything on schedule, but there is never enough time to do everything that's expected of them. They feel they have too many responsibilities and not enough time.

Thirteen-year-old Glenn often wonders whether his mother really likes working. "She seems frazzled all the time," Glenn says. "She never has time to relax, even on ·her day off. She used to go out with friends a lot and even do volunteer work, but not any more. There is never any free time. She's always in a hurry, but she still doesn't have time to do everything she wants to. My mother must run on nervous energy, and she makes me nervous, too.

"I feel stressed, too. I've got more homework than ever, and now I've got more chores at home because Mom went back to work. Mom's right; there just isn't enough time!"

When the whole family is under pressure, it's important to get back to discussing and planning. Everyone in the family can work ·together to help. You may feel there is no time, but one hour devoted to planning ·can save many hours of frustration in the future, and maybe save your sanity, too.

There are a few simple ways you can try to reduce the stress you and your family are feeling.

- Stop trying to be perfect at work or at home. Parents and teenagers should remember that no parent is perfect, everyone makes some mistakes, and everyone has a bad day now and then.

- Show some affection toward each other. After you work hard on a task—whether it is for school or home—it feels good to get a hug or a pat on the back. Also, try a few words, a note, or a phone call that says, "I care." You like to get these gestures from your parent, and your parent likes to get them from you, too.
- Get support from people outside the family, such as teachers, friends, and relatives. When others show signs of interest, respect, and affection, it builds feelings of warmth and security and reduces feelings of tension.
- Give and take, cooperate. Cooperation among family members also helps to reduce stress. In Peter's family, the children respect the parents' needs just as much as the parents respect the children's needs. "Mom calls it 'give and take.' I just call it 'good vibes'," Peter says.
- Do something to unwind when you come home from school and when your parent comes home from work. Have a snack; discuss the day's events. If someone comes home in a bad mood or exhausted, other family members should be reassured that they are not the cause of that unhappiness.
- Plan some family time each week—even if it's just you and your mom—to discuss problems and do things together.
- Take time for recreation, by yourself and with your family. Treat yourself to something you like to do, whether it's shooting baskets with friends, reading mysteries, or painting. Physical exercise not only relieves stress, it's good for you. Creative activities build your self-esteem.
- Emphasize your accomplishments rather than your

failures. Family members should take time to share success stories from school and work.

• Discuss problems, too. If parents have had problems at work that they settled successfully, they should discuss them with the family and show how they were handled. In this way, everyone can learn how to take care of problems better. Sharing helps parents and children feel better about their own problems.

• Establish priorities and focus on who and what is important.

• Have a sense of humor—that's most important of all!

Stress is often the result of feeling overwhelmed by too many, often conflicting, responsibilities. You and your parents should take a good look at what's expected of you and decide what responsibilities you can realistically handle. Set priorities. This will give you a feeling of control, an important factor in controlling stress.

When you establish priorities, you have to think of yourself and your family first.

When Fred and Brenda's mother first started to work, there was a lot of tension. "Boy, did we have stress!" seventeen-year-old Fred says. "Who's responsible for what? It took a lot of adjustment; it had to evolve. But we worked it out. We now have an understanding. We are equal partners, and we share the responsibilities of taking care of the house."

DEALING WITH GUILT

Family cooperation and sharing help to reduce stress in the family. It also helps to ease another strong emotion your mother is feeling. That emotion is maternal guilt.

If your mother is going back to work after staying at home with her children since they were born, she is probably going to experience some maternal guilt. What are these feelings, and what causes them? What do you do or say that might push your mother's "guilt button"?

It would be natural for your mother to feel some guilt at some time. She may question whether she is doing the right thing. She might be asking herself: Did I make the right decision? She may wonder, Am I a bad mother because I'm out working?

"Mothers perpetually feel guilty," says social worker Joan Olin. "They are always asking themselves, Am I doing the right thing? Is it bad for my child? They often feel that they are not getting support from their family or workplace. There is no way around guilt feelings. A mother always feels she should be doing more."

Sometimes the things you or other family members say to your mom will set off her guilt. Here are a few examples:

- *You don't spend enough time with me.* No working parent—mother or father—ever does spend enough time with the children. It's the *way* your family spends the time together that's important. Try to set aside some time each day, even if it's just a few minutes, when the family can get together and talk or take part in some activity.
- *You used to do lots of things for me, and you don't anymore.*
- *You never help me with my homework.* Plan a time when your parent can help you with your homework. While you're at it, discuss how much

help you should be getting from your parent. Should you be doing more on your own? Should you have better work habits?

- *The house is a mess.* The family must work together to keep the house clean.
- *You don't cook anymore. There's nothing to eat around here.* Your family should work together to do the menu planning, the shopping, and the cooking.
- *Didn't you do the laundry?* You can do your own laundry—and help with the rest of the family's.
- *We don't celebrate holidays the way we used to.* No family does as the children grow older.
- *A "real mother" would give me a ride to the game.* You can arrange for transportation. Perhaps your mother can share the driving with another parent.
- *Kwan's mom is always home after school.*
- *Vito's mother was at practice today.* Arrange for your mom to attend a practice when she's not working.
- *I'll never work when I have children. I'll never let my wife work.*

The way you act might set off your mom's guilt too.

- You pretend to be sick.
- You act angry or unhappy and try to make Mom think it's her fault.
- You pretend you're not listening when your mother talks to you.
- You turn to unacceptable behavior such as drugs and alcohol to try to get your parent to stop working.

The things you say or do that push your mom's guilt button are not productive. Talk things over with your mom and come to an agreement about what you want and what she can do for you. By planning and working together, you and your mom might be able to work out a schedule that allows her to do more of the things you want, while she still takes care of the things that are important to her.

Other people in your mother's life or even society, itself, might push that guilt button, too. Attitudes are changing slowly, but society has been telling us that child care is the working mother's problem. We still hear people say that working mothers should continue to take care of everything themselves.

In her workplace, your mother might be told, "You can work, but we don't want to hear about your problems at home." She may be getting criticism from her friends who don't work outside the home, who tell her what she should or should not be doing.

Your grandmothers or your mother's aunts belong to an older generation. They may never have worked, and they can be critical of your mother. They may accuse her of being selfish. Grandparents may say, "I never worked when I was raising my children."

Because of guilt feelings, mothers often think they are to blame for all of the problems, no matter what the cause. They feel bad if they can't stay home when children are sick, if they send the children to school when they are a little sick, or can't pick them up if they get sick at school.

Zack Turner's mom did feel guilty when she went back to work. "Zack gets so nervous before he takes a test or has to give an oral report, he almost gets sick," Mrs.

Turner says. "I used to think that if I stayed home he would be all right. However, our doctor finally helped me realize that Zack's nervousness had nothing to do with my going to work."

On the other hand, Jenny O'Neal's mother never felt guilty about going back to work. "Actually, I felt entitled to work," Jenny's mother says. "I wanted to stay home when my children were little. But now that they are in high school, I'm ready to go to work—and without guilt!"

"I was always in favor of my wife's working," Mr. O'Neal says. "I would have felt guilty if she hadn't gone back to work."

To avoid feeling guilty, your parent should evaluate her reasons for working, compare the benefits and the drawbacks, discuss it with her family, and think it through. She should then choose the best option. No one should feel guilty about picking the best option.

Mothers must be objective, decide what they want, and consider their own needs. They can be more productive when they have a positive attitude.

If your mother has guilt feelings, she should look at the source of these feelings objectively. Guilt often masks other feelings, such as anger or envy. If your mom feels guilty because she's not getting certain things done around the house, the family can help. Help your mother from going to the other extreme and letting guilt feelings make her do even more work at home. Don't let her give gifts excessively or give up all her own free time.

You will experience a combination of feelings, some positive, some negative. Don't let your feelings of frustration, anger, or stress get you into trouble. Channel them into constructive action.

You and your parents need to decide whether the emotions you are feeling can be resolved within the family, or whether you need the professional help of a coun-selor or social worker. Often, the whole family can work together to reduce stress and guilt by talking and planning. In fact, talking and planning will help reduce many different negative feelings. Planning can help relieve stress by reducing the pressures on each family member. Talking things over can help ease your mom's guilt feelings. After your family starts working together, you'll find that everyone's emotions calm down quite a bit.

CHAPTER ◇ 7

It's Not Such a
Great Idea

You, your parent, and your sisters and brothers
experience a lot of heightened, and mixed,
emotions when your parent goes back to work.
You may feel happiness, relief, and increased self-esteem.
At the same time, you may feel guilty, stressed out,
fearful, and angry.

There will be other things that you consider unwelcome
aspects in your life. Some things will make you say, "This
is not such a great idea after all."

Your parents have explained to you the reasons your
mother or father is going back to work. The family has
planned well. Still, difficult situations can and do come
up. What are some of the negative aspects of a parent's
going back to work, and what can you do to reduce or
eliminate some of them?

You may have a lot of changes in your life that you don't

like. Your parent is not at home as much as before. When she is home, she is often tired or preoccupied. Your parents make greater demands on you, asking you to do more around the house and to take more responsibility. They may ask you to make sacrifices such as giving up some of your social life in order to help out at home. You may even have to move because of a parent's new job and be separated from your friends and school.

HOME ALONE

After your parent goes back to work, she is not at home as much as before, and that makes a big difference in your life. You may be spending more time by yourself, and you may consider that a negative. You leave for school after your parents have gone to work and come home before they do. It can be boring, lonely, or frightening. You were used to having your mom or dad around to do things with you and for you.

Your parent may have to travel on business or work nights or weekends, which leaves even less time for you.

If you think of time alone as a negative, try turning it into a positive. You can use the time to do those things that you can accomplish by yourself. You can take care of some of your responsibilities, such as housecleaning or homework. You can also do some creative or recreational activities, such as exercise, painting, reading for pleasure, or whatever is fun for you.

Some kids need their mother around more than other kids do. When thirteen-year-old Lynette and her ten-year-old brother Robby came home from school, their mother was at work. Robby didn't seem to mind at all. He didn't need his mother's attention, and he didn't need Lynette's attention, either. He was happy working on his many hobbies, building a model racing car, or sorting his baseball card collection.

On the other hand, Lynette was very unhappy with the situation. Her mother had never worked outside the home before. She had always been there when Lynette came home from school. They had always had things to do together.

Now Lynette felt lonely. She missed her mother. She wasn't interested in doing anything by herself or with Robby. Most of the time she would go to her room and try to do some homework. Sometimes she cried.

Lynette was too embarrassed to tell her mother how she felt. Here was her younger brother, perfectly content with the way things were. But she hated it. How could she tell her mother? She didn't want her mother to think she was a baby.

The first thing Lynette should do is talk to her mother. Although she is embarrassed about her feelings, Lynette should let her mother know how she feels. Then she and her mother can work together to make things better for Lynette. They can figure out what Lynette can do or where she can go after school that would make her happier.

Maybe being alone does not seem like such a bad situation to you. Having some time to yourself might help you feel independent and mature.

When Reggie Miller was in junior high school, he had it pretty good at home. His mother volunteered as a teacher's aide at the local elementary school, but she was always there when Reggie was home. She did all the housework, the laundry, and the cooking.

Best of all, in Reggie's mind, was the way his mother helped him with his homework. Because she was a teacher's aide, she was especially good at this. She never gave Reggie the answers, but she would sit down with him and help him work out problems so he really knew what he was doing.

"I guess I didn't exactly appreciate what a great position I was in," Reggie admits. "It just felt normal to me. It was the way things had always been done."

Then, when Reggie entered high school, things changed. Reggie's mother decided she wanted to be a full-time teacher. Reggie was enthusiastic about the idea. His mother had to go back to the local community college and take a few extra courses in order to get her teaching certificate. She was lucky enough to find a good teaching job not too far from home.

Reggie and his mother talked about the changes that would take place when she went to school and when she started working. They planned for everything that needed to be done around the house. Everything sounded good.

So it's no wonder Reggie was surprised when things did not turn out as well as he had hoped. "I don't mind doing my share of the housework. We worked that out all right," Reggie says. "What I don't like is Mom's being out of the house so much. In the morning, she leaves before I do. When I come home from school, she isn't here. When she is at home, Mom doesn't pay much attention to me. She is too tired, and she still has to do her own homework or correct her students' homework."

Reggie thought it was ironic. Now that his mom was a teacher, she didn't have the time or the energy to help her own son with his homework. "I once thought it was a great idea that Mom would be a teacher. Now I'm not so sure."

For a parent, going to school in order to go back to work is time-consuming and tiring. If your parent is working and going to school, too, that's like a one-two punch! Reggie's mother had to go back to school before she could go back to work as a teacher. She needed to learn about all the new teaching methods that had developed since she was a teacher twenty years ago. "Going back to school was even tougher than going back to work," Mrs. Miller says.

Reggie agrees. "When Mom was in school, I saw her even less than I do now. And I don't see her very much now."

ATTENTION, PLEASE!

You are adjusting to a new lifestyle, and your parent is, too. Your parent must make changes. She has new and different responsibilities that demand her attention. As she adjusts to her new routines at home and at work, she may seem preoccupied. So, even when your parent is home, it may seem as if she is not paying much attention to you.

Besides being preoccupied with the changes in her life, your parent may be tired all the time. You might find that—especially when your parent first goes back to work—she is so tired at the end of the day that she can't do much of anything. She won't have enough energy to interact with the family or to pay as much attention to you as she once did.

You can help. You can do some of the work your parent once did around the house, such as getting dinner started. Then your parent may be less tired later in the evening. The family can do some activity together, and everyone will get more attention.

DEALING WITH CHANGE

For some teenagers, time alone is seen as a positive. For others, it is a negative. Some teenagers can't manage the changes in their lives or being on their own when a parent is working.

Some, teenagers react negatively to the changes that occur after a parent goes back to work. They may defy their parents and rebel against them by breaking the rules their parents set up and doing things they are not supposed to do.

There are teens who are just not mature enough to spend a lot of time on their own. Some teens can't function on their own. They don't know the boundaries of right and wrong. They need adult supervision. Teens who are not ready to be on their own need to enroll in programs where they have adult supervision. Or they can arrange to go to the home of friends, neighbors, or relatives where an adult is present.

You may feel that you are mature enough to function on your own. At the same time, you may not feel you are ready to assume the extra responsibilities you have to take on.

If you feel that your parents have assigned you too many responsibilities, talk it over with them. They might not realize what your difficulties are. Teenagers should not be asked to do too much or to do jobs that are not appropriate to their age or level of emotional maturity.

In some families, the oldest daughter becomes the parent figure when both parents are working. She may be given too much responsibility for caring for the house, the meals, and younger children. Whether you are male or female, if you feel that you have been given an unfair amount of work or responsibility, it is time to talk to your parent and come to an agreement that is more fair.

Best friends Carly and Erica were walking home after getting off the school bus. "Did you see that history assignment?" Carly asked. "I've never had to read so many pages in one night. I don't know when I'll get it done."

"Why don't you come over to my house, and we'll start it right now," Erica suggested.

"I can't. I've got to go home and baby-sit for my little brother, Lee. I also have to clean up the breakfast dishes and start dinner."

"What about your brother Tim. He's old enough to baby-sit. Doesn't he help?" Erica asked.

"No. He has basketball practice. Anyway, Mom says because I'm a girl I should be doing things at home."

"That doesn't sound fair to me. I share those kinds of jobs with my brother. Tonight it's his turn, and tomorrow I have to do it. You should talk to your mom."

"You're right," Carly said. "Tim should be doing his fair share."

When planning household tasks, the key words are "be fair and share." Even when chores are given out fairly, you may have to make some adjustments. If you have to be home to help with the housework, cook some of the meals, or care for a younger child, you may have to find other ways to participate in your usual activities, such as sports. If you talk to your friends, check the newspaper ads, and generally ask around, you'll probably be pleasantly surprised at how you can find fun things to participate in.

Your parent will have to make some adjustments, too. She won't be able to pursue all the activities she once did. She may have to rearrange her social life.

You are certainly not going to think it is fair if you have so many obligations at home that you have little or no time to spend on your own interests or being with friends. Teenagers need time to spend with friends and to pursue their own interests.

If a parent is reluctant to let you have a friend over when he or she is not at home, you can try negotiating. Perhaps you can have a friend visit if you agree to certain restrictions, such as limiting the number of friends that can come, the length of their visit, or what activities you can engage in.

ON THE MOVE

Your family may have to move to another part of your city or to another city to be closer to a parent's job. This will be a major change in your life. Try not to think of it as a totally negative change. It is very painful, but make definite plans to keep in touch with those to whom you feel closest.

MONEY PROBLEMS

Sometimes when a parent goes back to work—such as when a mother works to supplement the father's income, or when a mother goes from welfare to work—the family income increases. On the other hand, if the parent goes back to work following a divorce or the death of the other parent, there is less money.

You and your parent can cut down on the extra expenses, such as movies, cassette tapes, and eating out. You should study how to economize on basic necessities such as heat and food.

Consider getting your own part-time job. You would not only earn some spending money, but you would get an important taste of the business world. It would also be a chance to make new friendships and meet interesting people.

CHAPTER 8

But It's Not Such a

Bad Idea, Either

When your parent first goes back to work, you may have a lot of negative feelings. You see your parent less; you get less of her attention. You have more responsibilities, and you can't seem to get to the things you like to do. Could there be anything good about a parent's going back to work?

Yes, there are some good points to a parent's going back to work. If you think of it as a new adventure in life, you will find that the good points outweigh the bad.

HAPPY DAYS

One of the first things you will notice after your parent has gone back to work is that he or she is a happier person than before. Most of the time, mothers who work outside home have higher self-esteem and a better attitude than when they stayed at home. Although they have more responsibilities, they are happier and have more self-confidence. The job may add some day-to-day stress to your mother's life, but she'll most likely feel less anxiety overall. She will probably look and feel better physically, too. By going back to work, your parent has added back many dimensions to her life. She'll be feeling more in control, and more able to help you achieve the things you want in life.

If your dad has been unemployed or disabled for a long period of time, he will be very glad to be going back to work. He will have feelings of renewed respect and self-esteem. He will have increased energy and enthusiasm.

You'll feel better, too, as fifteen-year-old Brian did after his mother went back to work.

"Mom really loves her work," Brian says. "She has something to do during the day which she really likes. She gets to meet new people, and she has made many new friends. Now she has a lot of interesting experiences she can share with the family. Dad says Mom is more like she used to be. She just is a more interesting person all around."

A parent who works feels more self-respect and self-esteem. Her mind is challenged by the work. A mother feels better about herself when she knows that she is making a contribution to the family income.

When Inez Rivera's mother started working as a full-time teacher, she felt that she was not only contributing to her family's welfare, but also to the community. "It seems to me I have made a real difference in the lives of the children I teach," Mrs. Rivera says. "It makes me feel good about myself."

There can be changes in a parent's physical appearance, too. "There were revolutionary changes in my mom's looks," sixteen-year-old Natalie reports. "Before Mom went back to work, she looked older than she was, more like a grandmother. She was almost forty pounds overweight. She didn't seem to care how she looked. It was embarrassing.

"After Mom started working in an office, she really woke up. Her job gave her confidence. She wanted to look good, too. She changed her hairstyle, and she started to lose weight. Now, she really looks good. I enjoy introducing her to my friends."

Adanna noticed many big changes in her mother after her mother went back to work. "My father was not married to my mother, and he left her when I was just a baby and my brother was three," Adanna says. "My mother had been on welfare ever since. I never even thought that Mom wanted to go to work. But when our minister told her about a program that trained welfare mothers to do computer work and then helped them get jobs, Mom was real excited.

"Mom began to change while she was going through training. When she was on welfare, she had always seemed a little depressed and discouraged. Sometimes she said, 'I can't do anything right.'

"Now, you can tell she feels good about herself. Now she says, 'Let me tell you what I did today.' She's also making a lot more money than we ever got from welfare, which we all like.

"Even though Mom is not doing as much for me and my brother as she used to, I'm glad she went back to work. She's proud of herself, and I'm proud of her, too."

A POSITIVE ROLE MODEL

"Before Mom went back to work, I was sort of worried about myself," Adanna continues. "A lot of my friends' mothers were on welfare, too. I wondered if I would wind up the same way. But, when Mom got her job at the bank using a computer, I felt better. It proved to me that whoever is determined to do something and work toward it will succeed."

Your working mother is a positive role model. She shows by her example how a woman can combine a career with motherhood. Both boys and girls benefit from this role model. You'll be influenced by your mother's example to try new things, to make an extra effort. Your mother did what she set out to do, even though it was not easy. Now you know that it's possible to do just about anything you want to. You can see that things can be accomplished with effort and foresight.

Lottie Smith's mother had not worked outside home since before Lottie was born. Lottie knew her mother had wanted to be a lawyer for many years. Becoming a lawyer would require several more years of school to get a law degree. Then there would be the long, tough hours in the office when Lottie's mother was the newest member of the law firm. But Mrs. Smith set out to accomplish this goal, and she succeeded.

This inspired Lottie. Because her mother had achieved a difficult goal, Lottie realized that almost anything is possible if you are resolved to do it. It takes determination, hard work, and courage, too. Lottie remembered that her mom had told her this a hundred times, but it didn't sink in until her mother had actually gone ahead and done it.

That was why, when the dance department of Lottie's

high school was planning an important dance program, Lottie volunteered to do all the choreography. She knew she was taking a big risk in giving so much time to one project. But she also knew it was possible because she wanted to do it.

Lottie's younger brother, Theo, set a goal, too. He wanted to make the varsity soccer team in his sophomore year in high school. That would take a lot of time before and after school for drill and practice. Both Lottie and Theo picked up their positive attitudes from their mother.

When mothers work, daughters get the message that they too can lead a full life. It gives them something to strive for. Both sons and daughters use their mothers as positive role models.

Children whose mothers have jobs or careers have a more positive attitude about women and work than do their friends whose mothers are not working. They are less likely to accept sex-role stereotyping. They appreciate working women. Sons grow up viewing men and women as equals. Children and teens see that Mom and Dad can share work inside and outside the home.

The children of working women are generally more flexible in their outlook on life and are able to accept change more readily. They are more open to new ideas, and they are more tolerant. They learn to adjust more quickly, and they develop mutual respect.

SELF-ESTEEM

When your parents go back to work, you will notice that they have increased self-esteem. Your new responsibilities and independence can raise your own self-esteem. Accepting challenges, being praised for a job well done, and contributing to the welfare of the family will help you feel good about yourself.

In his book *Familyhood: Nurturing the Values That Matter*, Dr. Lee Salk writes that children of all ages and in all types of family situations should "share the chores in order to develop a sense of their own capabilities and to gain a sense of importance within the family unit."*

Your accomplishments will definitely make you feel better about yourself. Your self-confidence will grow. Your parents will treat you more like an adult.

INDEPENDENCE

Time alone at home can be a wonderful experience. With no one to tell you what to do, you can experiment with creating order in your own mind. You have time to think. You can decide what to do with your free time. You already know that independence is an important part of a teenager's life.

Teenage twins Julie and Jeff have always been very independent for their age. Independence has been stressed in their family. They were used to doing a lot for themselves, and they started doing even more when their mother went back to work. They arranged for transportation when they needed to go someplace. They made up a schedule and agreed who would stay after school for sports and who would come home to start dinner, and on which days.

Having a working parent allows for more freedom for teenagers and more self-reliance. Children feel good

* Dr. Lee Salk, *Familyhood: Nurturing the Values That Matter* (New York: Simon & Schuster, 1992), p. 88.

about themselves knowing they are capable of doing things for themselves.

When you are home alone and must do a lot for yourself, you are learning responsibility. You may be asked to take care of certain household projects, such as getting meals started or doing the family laundry on a regular basis. You are able to handle many different situations; and in an emergency, you know whom to call for help.

Mrs. Holt still has tears in her eyes when she remembers the day her thirteen-year-old son, Harris, called an ambulance for her when she collapsed in the house. "It shows how self-reliant he is," Mrs. Holt says. "He not only takes care of himself, but he can take care of other people when an emergency arises."

Self-reliance and responsibility go along with independence. You will probably get some extra privileges, too. You may be asked to use the family car to do errands or drive the younger children to friends' houses or to appointments. Then, in return, you may be allowed to drive to school. This is a benefit that you can negotiate with your parents.

FAMILY TIES

If both your parents—or your single parent—are working, it may seem as if you almost never see them. But what may seem like a bad thing can be turned into a good situation. Even though you are not spending much time together, your family can try to make the time you do have together productive and valuable. Some people call that "quality time." The word productive doesn't necessarily mean "work." It's good and productive to learn how to relax—have fun together. That's important to keep in mind. Life is supposed to be enjoyable.

Before a parent goes back to work, your family needs to plan how the household is going to be maintained. You need to establish rules, write up schedules, and assign chores. So, right at the beginning, just cooperating with your parents on planning and scheduling can bring you closer together. It's also fun to do, because you won't feel so burdened down.

Before your parent went back to work, she was doing a lot for you. She still will, but in a different way. The children and teenagers in the family need to start doing things for the parents' and the family. The feeling of cooperation is a good feeling, a good result of parents' working.

Efforts at cooperation don't stop with household chores. Because free time or time together as a family will be more limited when your parents are working, you may discover more positive ways to spend that free time together. If both your parents are working, it may be financially possible for your family to take longer or more frequent vacations together.

A mother who works outside home makes an effort to have quality time with her family in the evening or on weekends. She tries hard to do that and often manages to spend the same number of hours with her children as a stay-at-home mom.

"It's the last thing I thought would happen in our family," sixteen-year-old Will says. "But Mom and Dad get along better now than they did before Mom went back to work. The whole family gets along better. I guess it's because we're really working at it now. We actually think about our relationships."

Will's mother agrees. "We take the time to support each other," she says. "We are building family bonds that will last forever."

If your mother is now working, you may be spending more time with your father than you did before your mother went back to work. You may develop a closer association with your father. If your father was unemployed for a while, and you built up a relationship with him, that relationship will certainly go on after he goes back to work. Just look for signs of tiredness, and give him a chance to unwind when he first comes home. Researchers have found that, when a mother works outside the home, the father may spend more time with his children than the father of a single-career family does.

If you have sisters or brothers, you may notice that you are all closer than you were before your parent went back to work. You need to cooperate to get housecleaning, cooking, laundry, and other things done around the house, and the result will be that you learn to trust and rely on each other.

Sometimes when a mother goes back to work, she seems to pay less attention to her children. This is a good thing, according to sixteen-year-old Lisa. "When my mom went back to work, I suddenly became very independent. Something I had wanted to be for years. And, because Mom was around the house less, we fought less, too."

Visit your parent's place of work, if it can be arranged. Angela's mother is a teacher. "I always enjoy hearing about Mom's class and what they are doing," Angela says. "The best thing is when I have a day off from school, and I can go with Mom to her school and meet the kids in her class."

Thirteen-year-old Daryl's mother is a paralegal in a law office. Daryl thinks his mother's workplace is fascinating, and he loves to visit it whenever he can. Daryl is sure he's going to be a paralegal or a lawyer when he's older.

GAINING SKILLS

As you and your parents make plans and assign responsibilities, you may discover new ways of doing things in the home. You may find more efficient ways to get household chores done or may even decide to eliminate some jobs. Your family can actually accomplish more than you did before your parent went back to work, because you're all working at it, organizing and planning.

You may be responsible for a lot more household chores than you were before. But even here there are some advantages you may not have thought of. By doing chores, you can learn new skills, learn to get a job done properly and promptly, and learn to follow instructions. It's not such a bad idea for you, your sisters and brothers, and your dad to improve domestic skills. Besides, a job well done can give a person a sense of satisfaction.

What you learn at home can translate into an outside job. Since Mark helped get dinner started and did some cooking on the weekends at home, it was a natural that his first job was cooking in a restaurant.

When Mrs. Porter went back to work, her fifteen-year-old daughter, Pamela, reluctantly agreed that she would baby-sit for her two younger sisters, Julia and Christine. She was reluctant because she knew that baby-sitting four days a week would interfere with her social life and her after-school activities.

At the same time, Pamela was flattered that her mother trusted her enough to want her to take care of her sisters, who were only five and eight years old. She liked the idea that she had an opportunity to learn how to be responsible for younger children.

Pamela's opportunity did pay off. A year after she

started working, Mrs. Porter decided she could afford to send Julia and Christine to a nearby day-care center. At the same time, Pamela applied for a paid position to help out after school in the day-care center.

Pamela was hired to work two days a week. The director was impressed with the experience Pamela had gained by baby-sitting for her younger sisters. So what had looked like a real disadvantage turned out to be a benefit for Pamela.

All working parents and their families will probably agree that there are some unpleasant aspects to a parent's going back to work. However, just working out those negatives is a positive move. By practicing problem-solving, you will be learning and applying new skills, such as planning, communication, and self-discipline.

You gain maturity, the ability to make decisions, responsibility, and self-respect. You learn how to get organized. You learn to be on time. And you can start to budget your money.

MORE MONEY

A definite advantage of a parent's going back to work is the possibility of having more money for the family to spend. Contributing to the family income boosts your parent's self-esteem, and it is a benefit for you, too. In many families, the extra money will be needed for everyday expenses such as food, clothing, and housing. In other households there may be money for some luxury items such as family vacations, better clothes, sports equipment, a better home, or money for college. Having more family income can raise your standard of living.

After her mother went back to work, seventeen-year-old Cynthia started to notice more new things around the house. "New items kept popping up in every room," Cynthia says. "They were extras, not just necessities. And, another good thing, because she has her own salary, Mom will be able to send me an allowance when I'm in college."

With the extra salary, you and your family may be able to afford some of the services that help make running a household easier. You may be able to take your laundry to a professional laundry or to a dry-cleaner. In Cynthia's family they were able to have a cleaning service help clean the house once a week.

Before Luis' mother went back to work, the family was on welfare. They were barely able to pay for necessities such as food. Now that she's working, Luis' mother doesn't have to worry as much about serving a decent meal or being on time with the rent. And Luis and his brother and sister have a little spending money, too.

When there is less concern about finances, there is bound to be less stress and tension among family members. If both your parents are getting a paycheck, your family has the security of knowing that if one parent loses the job, the other parent is still working.

If only one parent has been the income earner in the household, she or he may be very nervous about remaining employed. After the other parent goes back to work, there is less fear. Your parent can change jobs more easily. She or he may feel less pressure at work, and might be able to reduce or eliminate the need for overtime or a second job.

There should be some control over how a family's money is spent. If your family does not have a budget, this is a good time to start one. Make that part of your planning. Having additional money and then budgeting helps young people understand exactly what money is, and what it can do for people when used wisely.

CHAPTER ◇ 9

You Can Cope When Your Parent Goes Back to Work

You want your family to cope successfully when your parent goes back to work. Coping well is the result of good planning and setting of goals. You need to decide how you and your family will spend time together and how you will spend the time you are alone. You need to delegate responsibilities fairly to family members.

Most important of all—because all the other factors depend on it—you need to communicate well. Everything works together. Before you can cooperate, you need to plan. Before you can plan, you need to communicate.

COMMUNICATION

For a family to cope with any situation, one of the most important elements is communication. This is certainly true of a family whose parent has gone back to work. Teenagers and parents need to share their ideas and their feelings with each other.

Every phase of your life requires good communication. Whether you are planning, setting goals, deciding on family activities and responsibilities, or expressing your feelings, you and your family need to communicate. Talk things over, express your opinions, share your feelings, and listen to the opinions and feelings of everyone else in the family. Include younger sisters and brothers in your discussions.

It may seem as if a family with two working parents, or a single working parent, is just too busy to have time to talk. Author Caryl Waller Krueger* suggests several "Touch-Base Times," when parents and children have time to talk and to communicate. Some of those suggested times are:

- At breakfast
- During the day, by telephone
- In the evening, when everyone is home from work and school
- At dinner
- A special evening hour
- Bedtime

---

*Caryl Waller Krueger, *Working Parent/Happy Child* (Nashville: Abingdon Press, 1990), p. 23.

Your family can have a discussion at dinner on school nights so parents can keep in touch with what you and your siblings are doing in school. Even when parents aren't home a lot, they should take an interest in what their kids are doing. You should find out what your parents are doing at work, too.

Kim is a junior in high school. She has two younger brothers. "We usually hold family meetings right after dinner when everyone is home," Kim says. "Sometimes our family discussions get pretty loud and wild. That's because we were told to be real honest. We're supposed to let people know when we're angry, or when we feel we're being taken advantage of.

"Mom might be angry because one of the kids didn't do an assigned job. But then one of the kids will yell back about being overworked. It's funny because, even though it's loud and wild, we do get problems straightened out. We are communicating instead of holding our feelings in and just getting mad."

Just finding the time to communicate can seem almost impossible, especially if you have a single parent. That's the way Maury felt. "My mother works every day and sometimes at night," Maury says. "I like to hang out with my friends after school. So Mom and I hardly see each other. We don't have time for talking or planning or anything. She usually yells something at me just as she's leaving in the morning to take my little brother to school and get to her work. I know it's partly my fault because I'm almost never home when mom is.

"I suppose if we had dinner together once in a while, or had breakfast together on Sunday, we could talk and plan and maybe even do some things together. I guess we should try that."

Listening

Communicating is not just talking (or yelling!). It also means listening. Parents need to listen to their children; and children should listen to their parents' needs, hopes, and complaints, too. Try to listen in a positive way.

The whole family should take time away from reading or watching TV for family discussions. Plan to set aside a time when no one is distracted. Have your family discussions when everyone can be calm. Don't discuss important issues when everyone is rushed or tired, such as right after work. Bedtime or after dinner is a good time for a one-to-one conversation between parent and teenager.

At dinner, try not to discuss topics that cause friction. On the other hand, don't avoid talking about something important just because it makes you or your parents uncomfortable. Everyone in the family should be open and honest about problems. Don't place blame on yourself or others. You should realize that you can't solve every problem by yourself. But you certainly can help.

You and your family should respect everybody's point of view. Don't ignore or interrupt the person who is speaking. Give everyone a chance to talk. Don't judge feelings or opinions. Parents should not be judgmental. Try to understand the other person's point of view, and make it clear that you do.

Express your feelings without yelling, blaming, complaining, or insulting. Don't limit your conversations to criticism only. Don't dwell on the negative, and don't bring up past problems. Discuss each problem separately and on its own merits.

"When complications develop in our lives, the family meet and discuss a solution," fourteen-year-old Phil says. "I think Mom is exaggerating just a little, but she says there are no problems that can't be solved when we sit down to discuss them."

You should be able to talk with your parents about anything that is bothering you. For instance, if you are uncomfortable about being home alone, or if you think you were given an unfair amount of housework to do, let your parents know how you feel.

Discuss the family rules you don't like. What is the reason for a rule? If you eliminate the reason, can you eliminate the rule, too? For instance, if your mom won't allow you to eat in the living room when you watch television because it gets too messy, promise that you will clean up afterward.

An Everyday Event

Family talks should be a regular event, not just when there is a crisis. Every day you should talk about the news—your own news as well as the world news—problems, ideas, and questions. This is a good time to discuss upcoming events and weekend plans and get everyone's opinion.

You can have an informal family discussion daily, and a more structured family meeting once a week. Mealtimes are the best times for the whole family to get together. While you and your parents are doing the dishes or at bedtime are also good times to talk. Both parents and children should talk about news of the day, up-coming events, and even some minor problems.

Sixteen-year-old Stacey laughs when she says that communicating seems to come naturally to their family. "After all, both my parents are lawyers. They love to talk. I think my brother and I inherited that trait. Before Mom went back to school, we used to have great discussions at dinner. We still do, except now we have to wait longer for dinner because Mom and Dad both get home pretty late. Mom insists that we have dinner together at least three times a week.

"We also have family meetings to discuss the big stuff, like when my parents were thinking about moving. We also have something called 'snuggle time' from nine to ten at night before we go to bed. That's when we talk about what happened during the day."

During family meetings, you can discuss topics such as housework, rules, and family activities. You also need to talk about your feelings. When a parent first goes back to work, feelings and emotions are heightened for all of you. This is a period of mixed feelings. Some things you like, some you don't. First you must recognize all your different feelings. Then you need to let your parents know how you feel.

Let your parents know how you feel, and listen to their points of view, too. Parent's should be encouraged to talk about their work, their successes and complaints. You and your sisters and brothers can talk about problems and accomplishments, school and friends. As part of your family discussion, you may ask your parents how they felt when they were your age.

If you find it difficult to talk about feelings, try writing them down before you discuss them. Keep the lines of communication open. Everyone's feelings are important. This is a growing time for everyone in the family.

Communicating By Phone

When a parent goes back to work, the family can put the phone to good use.

The amount of time a parent can devote to a child's phone call will depend on his or her work situation. You may only be able to make a quick call to say hello and that you're home from school. If you have news to share, it may have to wait until dinner. Your parent may not be able to take calls at work. In that case, you may have to call another adult, a relative or neighbor.

When planning and setting up household rules, establish some guidelines on the frequency of calls you make and who can be called. Everyone in the family, including the very young children, should know mother's and father's work phone numbers. On your phone list, have the numbers of people who can be called if your parents can't be reached. Besides communicating by phone, you and your parents can leave notes or recorded messages for each other.

School and Work

When your parent first goes back to work, the new situation might distract you so that you don't do as well in school for a few days, or you might have trouble with homework. Your teachers should be notified about the change, just as they should know about any big changes in your life. This way they will understand that you are going through some stress.

Encourage your parents to take an interest in your school work and homework. Ask them to attend school meetings and conferences. They should meet your teachers, if possible. Then, when you tell them about successes or problems in school, your parents will have a better understanding of what you're talking about.

In the same way, you should try to visit your parent's

workplace occasionally. Get an idea of the work your parent does. Meet some of her coworkers.

Thirteen-year-old Rashid Randolph and his mother live in an area of the city where there has been some violence against people of color. Mrs. Randolph is very worried about Rashid being home alone after school or on school vacation days. Because the school is close to Mrs. Randolph's office, she tells Rashid to come to her office after school a few times a week instead of going directly home.

Rashid enjoys going to his mother's office. He can do his homework there or read. A lot of his mother's coworkers know him now, and often he helps them by running errands.

LONG-TERM PLANNING

You need to think of short-term and long-term planning.

Planning for the short term, your family will be thinking of the day-to-day practicalities: how to handle housework, child care, and family activities.

For the longer term, you and your family need to set goals. Each member of the family will have different goals. For you, it may be getting good grades in high school so you can get into the college of your choice. For a younger brother or sister, it may be making the soccer team or reading fun and interesting books over the summer. Of course, your parents have goals, too.

There are family goals and individual goals. Everyone in the family helps each other achieve those goals. You should think about what's involved to reach your personal goals.

Ask yourself, "Where do I want to go? What steps are needed to achieve my goals? What are acceptable alternatives to my goals? What are my priorities?" Be sure to share your plans with your family, and listen to their plans, too.

If you live in an area where there is violence and drug use, or if some of your friends or an older sister or brother has dropped out of school, you may feel discouraged about your future. Why even bother setting goals? you may ask. If you have ambitious, but realistic goals, you can achieve them. Your parent went back to work, so you know goals can be realized. The only secret to anyone's success is the systematic gathering of knowledge, combined with practicing to make the skills truly a part of you.

When you think about your future, dream a little. That may give you an idea of what you would like to do in the future.

Seek out positive places and positive people that build your self-esteem. Gangs contradict self-esteem; they don't affirm you as a person, they use you.

You can build your own self-esteem and vision for the future by sharing your parents' successes with them. Ask your parent to share his or her feelings of self-esteem. When your mother finishes a difficult project, how does she feel? If your dad is complimented by his boss, what does it mean to him?

FAMILY FINANCES

In addition to planning household tasks and setting personal goals, you need to plan your finances. Whether there is now more family income, or less, your family should set up a budget that everyone understands. You can make up your own personal budget or financial plan, too. Learning to budget, and being responsible for sticking to the budget, are great preparation for the time when you will have your own household.

Some experts say that the children of divorced or single parents have a better understanding of how to use money. Garrett quickly learned about budgeting after his parents were divorced. Sometimes his dad sent money, but most of the time Garrett and his mother had to live off of her income alone. When his mother showed him that her monthly income would just about pay for food, rent, electricity, and phone, he realized that the budget would not allow for the new sports equipment he wanted.

If your family was not budgeting their money before your parent went back to work, you should make up a budget now. Decide what the family expenses are—not just basic necessities such as food and rent, but also recreation and entertainment—and how much of the family income will be allotted to each item. Set priorities and limits. Get a book on budgeting from the library to help you.

Family income does not always increase when a parent goes back to work. That makes budgeting especially important.

Find out what your parent can or cannot afford. Ask for an explanation, so that you can take part in allocating money. You'll be amazed, once you look into it, how well you can do if you change a few shopping habits. For example, you can start by not buying packaged foods from the supermarket. When you compare what you are getting, pound for pound, you'll realize that the convenience foods, or meals in a package, are costing many times per pound more than you would pay buying fresh and cooking from scratch. Figure out your savings over a month's time, and you'll probably feel encouraged to make more things yourselves.

Do you need to get a job in order to have the money you need for the things you want? Will you get an allowance?

Whether you earn money by working or get an allowance, you should be allowed to decide how to spend your own money. This is important training for you. If you make mistakes, just evaluate them and learn for the future. Don't get upset about it. You should have a personal budget or financial plan, too. However, you shouldn't have to worry about the family's finances; that is an adult responsibility.

COOPERATION

As you grow up, you discover that the special relationship between you and your sisters and brothers and your parent changes and grows with all of you. You have depended on your parents for many things. Now, they need to depend on you for some things. This is especially true if both parents are working, or if your single parent is working. Everyone needs to take extra care to cooperate, so that life can be more fun for everyone.

When a parent goes back to work, it's important for every member of the family to cooperate for the good of the family. Fifteen-year-old Wade thinks of his family as a team. "Everyone needs to work together," he says. "We expect everyone to help out, whether they want to or not, even my younger brother and sister."

Wade's mother agrees. "When you go back to work, you need a supportive family. Everyone works hard so no one is singled out or treated unfairly," she says.

Even if you have a single or divorced parent, your family can be a team. Every member of the family in the household is on the team; and, just like a well-trained football squad, each family member has an "assignment," a job to be responsible for. You're not just helping out one team member by doing your job, you are participating in a team effort for everyone's benefit. No one is better or more important than the others. Everybody pulls their own weight. As Wade likes to say, "We're all in the same boat—and it isn't the Titanic!"

With work or school, extracurricular activities, housework, and social activities, you and your parents have busy schedules. You should all have mutual respect for each other's schedules. Plan together so there are no surprises. If you want something done for a special occasion, or if your parents want you to stay home and do something for them, you need to plan, communicate, and cooperate with each other.

Getting organized and coping when a parent goes back to work is not an easy task. As a teenager, you are going through a period of transition. When your parent goes back to work, it is also a time of transition. Like other teens, you are moving up. You can make decisions and be depended upon. You can take responsibility and command respect for your decisions.

Of course, teens are capable of accepting different amounts of responsibility as they grow older. And not every thirteen-year-old or seventeen-year-old is ready for the same degree of self-reliance. All parents should know their children and how much responsibility they can handle.

In the Yang family, fifteen-year-old Lynn and her thirteen-year-old brother Dan are given a lot of independence and responsibility by their mother. "I believe a parent should have faith in her children," Mrs. Yang says. "They rise or fall according to expectations. My children are given an opportunity on a daily basis to test themselves. They don't always succeed, but they survive."

COMPROMISE

Sometimes coping requires compromise. Occasionally, a parent or teen has to give up or modify their desires for the general good of the whole family. It may mean you have to give up some of your activities or social life. It may mean a parent has to take a less demanding job.

Ellen didn't have to give up all of her after-school activities because of her mother's work. But sometimes it was necessary to miss a practice or meeting in order to help her mother out or take care of her younger brother. "If anything came up, I usually had enough advance notice to tell my advisor or coach," Ellen says.

FAMILY TIME

Your family is communicating, planning, and cooperating so all of you can take care of the necessary housework and succeed at school and on the job. It is important to plan your free time, too.

A good deal of time away from work should be family time. Time spent together provides emotional support, and most families like to be together.

In his book, *Familyhood: Nurturing the Values That Matter*, Dr. Lee Salk suggests that parents make an appointment to spend time with one child at a time. A teenager should also make appointments with friends.

Your family needs to plan leisure time, including weekends, just as you plan the housework. Arrange to have some unscheduled free time for the family to do "nothing" together at home.

All family members can use some time to themselves, too. You probably need to be alone to unwind and digest your experiences after a busy schedule in school. Your parents also need to be by themselves, and to be able to see their friends.

Although your family may only be able to have short periods of time together during the week, there are many ways that you can spend that time. What you do will depend upon the ages, interests, and skills of each member of the family. Discuss ideas and listen to everyone's suggestions. Here are a few ideas to start with:

- Set aside a period for everyone to read; go to the library together.
- Attend concerts or plays (community plays and concerts cost less).
- Exercise or jog together.
- Play games together, indoors or outdoors, evenings or weekends; try playing board games.
- Work on a project such as woodworking or model-building.
- Participate in sports: parents and children—including teens—playing together; parents watching and children playing (or visa versa); or attending a spectator sport as a family. Amateur, high school, or college sporting events will cost less than professional sports; some may even be free. Parents should occasionally try to attend their children's sports practice sessions during the week, not just Saturday's big game.

Now that his parents are divorced, the one thing Garrett misses most is having his dad coming to his soccer practice and games. Garrett's mother tries to come to as many as she can. "I know it's hard for Mom to get to the games, especially since she has to work on some Saturdays,"

Garrett says. "I think it's great when she can come. I have my family there cheering for me, and I feel better."

When parents are working, it is difficult to find time for the family to be together. Mealtime may be the only opportunity. Everyone in the family can do something to help plan and prepare meals. The family should make an effort to be together for breakfast or dinner at least a few times a week.

When your family has dinner, don't rush through the meal. Keep the television turned off. Don't just eat together, but make the meal preparation a group effort, too.

Spend time together before dinner. Relax together and enjoy a snack before dinner. This is time to unwind and to talk, while you also reduce hunger pangs. It's nice for you and your parents to have some quiet time before dinner.

Try to arrange some one-to-one time with a parent after dinner. Your parent can help you with your homework by proofreading papers, giving you quizzes, or testing you on your vocabulary.

For sixteen-year-old Gloria, family comes first. "Because our family can't get together too much, we always have dinner together," Gloria explains. "And we clean up together, too. Friends and other activities come after that. Sometimes I wish I could be with my friends. But I usually don't mind too much. Our family always has a lot of fun at the dinner table."

Weekends are not just for chores. It's a great opportunity for the family to be together over an extended period of time.

If your parents are divorced, you can work out a way to share time with each of them. Just discuss it, and don't get upset if one or the other seems to feel rejected. These feelings are normal, and they will pass.

You might consider the following family projects for weekends:

- Shop for food and do other household chores together.
- Wash the car together.
- Go on picnics or take camping trips.
- Visit museums. (If you live in the city, you may find that there is a special bus going to museums on weekends.)
- Attend concerts, movies, or plays.
- Participate in religious events.

Vacations are a good time for families to be together. Everyone in the family can help plan the vacation. Each one should be able to suggest where to go and what to do. Discuss the length of time you'll have. Allow for returning early enough to rest before going back to your normal activities. You can have fun together, seeing what you can do with the amount of money the family can spare for this vacation.

Have some "family rituals" in the daily and weekly routine. Family rituals are those things your parents and you always do together; or they may be things your parents did with their parents and want to continue. You can celebrate religious holidays and maintain other family traditions.

A very satisfying activity for parents and teens is doing charitable work together. Your religious organization or community center may need people to help serve meals to the hungry, gather clothing for the needy, or help out with fund-raising events.

For the second year in a row, the Johnson family volunteered to help at the Community Center's holiday bazaar. Donna, fifteen, played the piano, and her thirteen-year-old brother, Arthur, played the trumpet to entertain the shoppers. Her younger sister, Jasmine, helped sell raffle tickets; and her mom and dad waited on tables in the lunch room.

At the end of the day, the five Johnsons sat at a table in the lunch room, exhausted, but happy. "I ache all over," Donna said, "but I really feel good. We helped the Community Center raise enough money for next year's programs, and it was great to do it with my family."

"Let's do it again next year," Jasmine suggested. The rest of the family laughed and nodded their heads in agreement.

Family time together should not be "forced fun," but should be planned so that everyone genuinely enjoys it. Get suggestions from all family members. Be sure there is time for love and family fun, not just discussing discipline. Try to watch less TV and talk to each other more.

Besides spending quality time with her family, a teen needs time to get together with friends and be involved in her own social activities. The family's social activities should vary.

COPING WHEN YOU HAVE TO MOVE

Sometimes in order for a parent to get a good job, the family must relocate to another city or state. There may be more need in other areas than your own for the type of work your parent does.

Moving often means leaving your school and your friends, everything that is familiar to you. Put these two factors together—your parent going back to work, and moving your household at the same time—and you have a major upheaval to deal with.

Everyone will have different feelings about moving. This is the time to communicate those feelings. Moving can be a traumatic experience for all of you. You will have to get used to a new school, meet new friends, and get started in new activities. It can be stressful for your parent, too. He or she may be as apprehensive about the move as about the new job.

Get involved in planning the move. Do some research. Collect information about the area you're moving to. Find out about its history and interesting sights. What's different about this new place? What's the same as the neighborhood you are living in now?

If possible, visit the new area before you move. You can learn about the community from the people who live there, leaders of a church or synagogue, or directors of the community center and other organizations. If you're lucky, you might have a relative or friend who lives in the new area, or even the friend of a friend. That person can show you around and introduce you to other people.

After you move, try to get into the same activities that you were involved in where you used to live. Try for as much consistency in your life as possible. It takes time to become part of a community. You need to take the initiative. Invite people to your home; don't wait for them to come to you. Parents, too, need to find new friends and activities to balance their lives.

Matt Wallace was happy when his dad announced that he was going back to work. Matt knew that his dad had been looking for a new job since he had been laid off from his factory job, so it was good news to hear that his dad found one.

Then came the bad news. In order to get a good job, Mr. Wallace told the company that he was willing to relocate. The new job he accepted was in another state, three hundred miles away!

Matt was going to be a junior in high school in the fall. He had planned on being a reporter for the school newspaper. Now all that was impossible. Matt would have to give it all up, not to mention leaving his friends, the soccer team, and that good third-year math teacher.

Matt mentioned the move to his history teacher, Mr. Griffith. "Why don't you do some research and find out about the history of that area," Mr. Griffith suggested.

Matt made a face. "I can't believe that place has anything interesting about it. There's only the factory where my dad is going to be working."

Mr. Griffith smiled. "I happen to know that an important battle of the Civil War took place near there. The community reenacts the battle every summer."

Following Mr. Griffith's advice, Matt read about the Civil War battle and about other interesting sights in the area. In fact, Matt became excited and anxious to see the actual battle site. He still wasn't crazy about moving, though.

What really surprised Matt was his dad's behavior. His dad seemed nervous and unhappy. "Dad, what's up?" Matt asked. "I thought you wanted to move, but you don't look too happy about it."

"I wanted this job, and that meant moving," Mr. Wallace said. "I know it's upsetting your life. It's upsetting my life, too. I just hope I made the right decision."

When they made the move, Matt was even more depressed. Their new apartment was smaller than the one they had lived in before, and the high school looked small and old. He found out that the school newspaper was not very good. But there was also some good news. The advisor for the school paper said they could use Matt's experience as a reporter.

It still wasn't easy for Matt. He didn't know anyone in the area, and he wanted to make friends. When the newspaper staff had a meeting, Matt invited them to his apartment, and he ordered pizza. Everyone met Matt's father and they enjoyed a few hours with each other. Matt also tried out for the soccer team and met some new friends that way.

Mr. Wallace was making friends, too. He met people at work who had children around Matt's age. The families got together to attend soccer games.

It took a while, but Matt and his dad adjusted to life in their new home.

ALTERNATIVES

In any situation that involves change and risk—such as a parent's going back to work—some plans may not work out exactly the way you thought they would. In our complex society new conditions keep presenting themselves, so we have to accept constant change. This doesn't mean you have to give up on your ideas, but you have to be ready to think creatively at a moment's notice to come up with alternative plans.

If you observe something in the family's plans that isn't working right, come up with some alternatives and discuss them with your family. Nothing is written in stone. Everyone in the family should be flexible and open-minded. Ideas can change and methods can change. Even if you helped plan your responsibilities in the family, you may find that you are being asked to do more than you expected.

Discuss with your family why a situation is a problem to

you. Is it a problem for the whole family or just one person? Make a list of alternatives to the situation. Decide which alternative might work best, and try it out. Let everyone in the family get in on the problem-solving. You never know who might have the best idea.

Don't ignore a problem. Do something about it. Coping doesn't mean your life will be problem-free. It does mean that when a difficult situation comes up, you do something about it.

As an alternative to working full time, some parents might be able to work in their homes. Home-based businesses are becoming more prevalent now that big businesses are offering less full-time employment. Some parents might be able to take jobs that do not require overtime, late meetings, or out-of-town trips. On the other hand, some parents find night jobs so they can be home with their children during the day. A parent could gradually work up to full-time employment by working part time to begin with, and going to school part time. Your family may need to hire someone to help with the housework or to care for younger children.

CHAPTER 10

Can Anybody Help?

So your parent is going back to work, and you and your family are doing everything "by the book." You are communicating, planning, and compromising, but things still aren't working out the way you would like them to. You may be wondering if this is the time to get some help. Family, friends, neighbors, community workers, and social workers are willing to help if you just ask.

The help you need may be something very simple, such as having someone to check in with by phone after school. A more complicated problem might require the help of a professional counselor. You may sometimes feel that you would like the advice of objective people outside of the family, such as teachers, school counselors, or social workers.

FAMILY

If some members of your extended family—such as a grandparent or an aunt or uncle—live nearby, they may be able to help your family. Even if relatives just call you or have you call them to be sure everything is all right at home, that is a help.

When Mrs. Kante found a job and had the chance to get off welfare, she was happy and excited. She was also worried about her fourteen-year-old son, Dennis. She didn't want him out on the streets after school with no planned activities, and she didn't want him to be home alone. Dennis had already been harassed by gang members in the neighborhood, and Mrs. Kante was concerned about his safety. Dennis and his mother lived with his grandmother, but Grandmother worked, too.

Mrs. Kante was relieved when Dennis' great-grandmother offered to have him come to her apartment after school. "I'll love having some company. He can watch TV here, do his homework, and help me do some things around here that are too hard for me now," Great-grandmother said.

Brent's grandmother is almost always available to help in case of an emergency. When Brent sprained his ankle during soccer practice, his grandmother drove him to the doctor. She stopped by to give Brent lunch and read to him when he was sick at home with the flu. "She calls herself the emergency grandma," Brent says.

FRIENDS AND NEIGHBORS

Brent is lucky to have a grandparent who lives nearby, drives a car, and is willing to help out. If you don't have grandparents that live near your home, you might be able to find friendship and help from an older couple or a single person, people who may have already raised families. They can be there to talk to, give some advice, help take care of younger children, and perhaps drive you places.

When Tanya is busy with school activities, her younger brother Seth goes to Mrs. Blake, a neighbor. Sometimes Tanya goes there after school, too. It seems as if Mrs. Blake always just happens to have a plate of home-made cookies ready for them. "Mrs. Blake is the greatest neighbor," Tanya says.

Mrs. Blake looks embarrassed when she answers, "I'm glad I can help out. It makes me feel needed. Otherwise, I would just sit at home and rust away."

Friends can be helpful to your family, too; your own friends as well as your parent's friends. If you have a friend or neighbor close to your age who has working parents, the two of you can share and compare ideas. You might be able to spend some of your free time at the friend's home, and your friend can spend time in your home, too.

If your neighbors are available to help out, it may be only on an informal basis. On the other hand, you might want to make that neighborly help more structured. You and your neighbors can get together and organize a block parents group or a neighborhood watch program. Block parent programs are planned for after-school hours. They provide for children to go to the home of a trained neighborhood volunteer in case of an emergency.

OUTSIDE HELP

Now that your parent has gone back to work, there may be some extra family income. This might mean that your parent is able to hire someone outside the family to help with the housework, child care, or other tasks.

Often the extra income is not enough to pay for outside help. If your family cannot pay for help, you can try bartering or trading tasks such as child care, cooking, or home repairs with neighbors or relatives. Troy, a senior in high school, didn't have time in his busy schedule to take care of his younger brother, Michael, after school. Troy's neighbor took care of Michael in exchange for Troy's washing all the windows in their neighbor's apartment. It was a job that was too difficult for her to do, and one that she couldn't afford to pay for.

PROFESSIONAL HELP

There may be long-standing problems between your parents that get worse when one of them goes back to work. It's also possible that some difficulties arise for you or a sister or brother. If communicating, planning, and compromising don't have a positive effect on problems, seek out professional help. Be very careful whom you ask for help. You don't want to ask for help from a negative-minded counselor, or someone who doesn't understand or respect your feelings. Go by your feelings about whether you trust this person's advice. Just remember, nobody knows you as well as you know yourself.

Talk to your school counselor. A doctor, social worker, or religious worker may be able to help with more serious problems.

"Whole families come to our office for counseling," says Tema Rosenblum, Family Life Educator and psychotherapist with the Jewish Family and Community Service in the Chicago area. "They already have anger because of other problems. When the mother goes back to work, it just adds one more problem."

IN THE COMMUNITY

Sometimes a family's needs go beyond what the help of friends, relatives, and neighbors can do. You can get help from schools, churches, park systems, social service agencies, sometimes even from your employer or your parent's employer. You need to do some research to find the group in your community that fits your needs best.

After-School Programs

According to the United States Department of Labor, Bureau of Labor Statistics, in the twenty years between 1970 and 1990, the percentage of children from two-parent families where both parents work almost doubled, going from 36 to 61 percent.* Many of the children in these families are teens and preteens.

There is growing attention to the need for after-school programs for teens and preteens. Organizations in many parts of the country are helping develop new programs.

If you join an after-school program, find one that offers a variety of experiences, including recreation, sports, and academic help. The program should provide for both physical activity and quiet time. It should provide the opportunity for youth to develop their skills and talents. Snacks should be available, and there should be time and space for kids to do homework.

A good program will have access to community resources such as ice-skating, swimming, libraries, youth organizations, and arts centers. Some programs offer trips to museums or zoos. In an after-school program, you can learn how to care for younger children, as well as having the chance to socialize with your peers (kids of your own age).

*U.S. Department of Labor, Bureau of Labor Statistics, *Working Women: A Chartbook*, Bulletin #2385, August, 1991.

After-school programs take place in public schools (sponsored by the school or a community group), non-profit or for-profit organizations, religious institutions, private schools, and government facilities. Some programs offer sports, arts, dramatic or dance activities, and computer classes. They may also include community involvement, social activities, board games, videos, computer games, hobbies, free time, and homework time.

When you and your parents are evaluating an after-school program, look for the following features:

- A staff that works well with the children and teenagers
- A chance for children and teenagers to be with children their own age, as well as adults and younger children
- A flexible schedule where participants can help plan activities and choose those that interest them
- A program that promotes appropriate behavior and includes participants in setting the rules
- A safe place that accommodates a variety of experiences, indoors and outdoors, physical activities as well as quiet time
- A program that provides a wide variety of activities for physical, mental, and emotional growth

In an after-school program, the young people should know the rules of behavior. They should be fair and clear. Teens should be able to participate in the development of these rules.

Thirteen-year-old Lana is glad she signed up for the after-school program at the community center. "At first I thought it was just for babies," Lana says, "but I made a lot of friends, and I feel safe there. It's better than being home by myself."

Do some investigating to find an after-school program that suits your family's needs. If you don't have one in your area, your parents might want to set one up with the help of others in your community. They can work with community and school leaders, the local parent-teacher organization, and other parents. At the end of this chapter is a list of organizations to contact for information.

You and your parent may agree that, since you are a teenager, you don't need an after-school program. That's what Barry Lovett's mother thinks. "Now that Barry is in junior high school, I think he's better off in scouting or one of the school clubs," Mrs. Lovett says. "He can come home or go to friends' homes, too. He doesn't need special programs."

You may not want or need an after-school program. However, if you are caring for younger school-age brothers and sisters, your family should consider a program for them. It might be too much of a burden for you at this time.

In an after-school program, children have a wide variety of activities to take part in. They can be with other children their own age.

Fourteen-year-old Kelly's younger brother Tony goes to an after-school club so Kelly is never given the responsibility of taking care of him. Kelly likes the arrangement because she doesn't have to give up her own after-school activities.

Tony likes it, too. He has friends who go to the after-school club. They play soccer when it's nice out, and board games indoors when the weather is bad. "I could never do those things if I went home with Kelly," Tony says. "Besides, Kelly is too bossy."

Telephone Helplines

Instead of participating in an after-school program, you might like a simple arrangement such as a check-in service. You can check in by phone with a professional counselor after school. You, your parents, and the counselor would agree in writing where you are allowed to go after school, when you should be home, and other arrangements.

Several cities around the country have services that provide telephone helplines. Teens can call helplines for advice and assistance when they can't reach their parents. These "hotlines" for children and teens at home alone provide both emotional and practical help. Telephone services have trained counselors to reassure you when you're at home alone, and they can offer occasional advice. Kids call for a variety of reasons: for advice in case of illness or accident; because they are frightened; or simply because they are bored.

Community Programs

If you are going to be staying home alone, there are other programs that can help you with potential problems. You can get training in first aid through the Red Cross. There are baby-sitters' classes to help you if you are caring for younger children. You can join a survival class to help you handle many different subjects, such as loneliness, safety tips, and cooking and nutrition. You can seek out special self-defense classes for girls. Girls and boys can go to classes like yoga or tai chi. Scouting groups can teach you a variety of skills.

Many classes can be found at the public library, community center, or right in school. In fact, your high school or junior high may have after-school clubs or classes in art, photography, or reading improvement.

Your local YMCA or community center may offer fitness classes, weight lifting, swimming or other sports. During summer vacation, community groups and schools have camp or summer school programs to fill a variety of needs and interests. Along with classes on first aid and baby-sitting, your public library has books for you and your parents on child care, household maintenance, creative activities, first aid and safety.

Do some research to find other programs in your community. Ask teachers, librarians, and community leaders:

- What programs for teenagers are offered in the community?
- Where do they take place?
- What age groups participate in these programs?
- Are there fees or other expenses involved, such as for a required uniform, textbook or supplies? Is there a scholarship to cover these expenses?
- What transportation is available to and from the program location?

There are classes for parents, too. These programs can provide ideas for the whole family to use. The local high school, college, or junior college may offer courses, as well as the community center, churches and synagogues.

Support Groups

There may be a parent support group in your neighborhood. These groups can be found at schools, community centers, or religious institutions. Your parents can form their own group with friends and neighbors. Working parents join together to share ideas and concerns. You can form your own support group with your friends. In these groups, you and your family can find out what works for other families. Sometimes the emotional support is the most important thing to be gained in such a group.

Your school's parent and teacher organization can also offer support to parents and teens. They can provide practical suggestions for problems all families face. There are support groups for single parents or divorced parents. Some support groups offer classes that teach working parents and their children how children can care for themselves safely and effectively. Many communities have "welcomers" clubs for people new to the area.

DO IT YOURSELF

When the programs and services you want are not offered, you can get the ball rolling and get them started yourself. If you see a need for a program at the school or in the community, campaign for it. Get friends and neighbors to help.

Sixteen-year-old Hannah Gilbert and her fourteen-year-old brother, Doug, were always busy after school. Hannah was on the girl's junior varsity soccer team. Doug was on the theater crew, always working on scenery for the next school play. The last school bus left much earlier than Hannah and Doug could leave, so their mother would pick them up every evening after school. Often Mrs. Gilbert would drive some of Hannah or Doug's friends who didn't have a ride home.

Then Mrs. Gilbert got a full-time job. She was not able to pick Hannah and Doug up from school any more. Hannah asked around and found out that many of her friends' mothers worked. They depended on other mothers to drive them home from school. Some mothers were driving as many as five teens home.

Once, there was no ride for Hannah and Doug; they had to take a taxi home. Hannah was frustrated and angry. "What we really need is a late bus to take all the kids home after activities," she told her mother.

"So, let's campaign for one," Mrs. Gilbert answered. "You remember how we campaigned to get the elementary school to start a lunch program when you were in the fifth grade. We can do it again."

Mrs. Gilbert talked to her friends. Many were working mothers, and some were not. They were all interested in having a late school bus to bring the kids home safely from after-school activities. Hannah and Doug got their friends together to help, too.

The group printed petitions and got as many signatures as they could from families in the community. Then Hannah and Doug, Mrs. Gilbert, and other parents presented their case—along with a stack of signed petitions—to the school board. They explained why a late bus was needed. They had researched the cost of having a bus every evening.

The school board discussed the idea and approved it. Hannah, Doug, their mother and their friends were excited, not only because they got the bus service they needed, but because they had achieved it themselves. They would have to pay a fee to get the extra bus, but that didn't seem to bother anyone. "It's a lot cheaper than taking a taxi home," Hannah said.

There are a lot of things you can do to cope with life's challenges when your parent goes back to work. You may have to get things started by finding out who can help, what programs are available in your community, and what programs are needed. Just remember, you're not alone in the world. Reach out to other people and to new people as often as possible. Keep looking for the positive side of every situation you encounter.

If you would like to get more information about after-school programs, contact the following organizations:

Catalyst
250 Park Avenue South
New York, NY 10003-1459
(212)777-8900

The Center for Early Adolescence
3 to 6 p.m. Project
University of North Carolina at Chapel Hill
Suite 223–Carr Mill Mall
Carrboro, NC 27510
(919)966-1148

Children's Defense Fund
122 C Street NW
Washington, DC 20001
(202)628-8787

The School-Age Child Care Project
Wellesley College
Center for Research on Women
Wellesley, MA 02181
(617)431-1453 ×2546

U.S. Department of Education
Office of Policy and Planning
400 Maryland Avenue, SW
Washington, DC 20202
(202)401-0590
(Send for a free copy of the report, "National Study of Before and After School Programs")

For information on setting up telephone helplines, contact:

PhoneFriend
P.O. Box 735
State College, PA 16804

For information on safety and other ideas for children or teens who stay home alone, contact:

Project Home Safe
1555 King Street
Alexandria, VA 22314
(800)252-SAFE
(703)706-4600

Project Latchkey
National Parent-Teachers Association
333 North Wabash Street
Chicago, IL 60611-9894
(312)951-6782
(312)549-3253 (to order material)

The following youth service organizations provide positive programs and activities for teenagers:

Alternatives, Inc.
1126 West Granville Street
Chicago, IL 60660
(312)973-5400

Big Brothers/Big Sisters of America
230 North 13th Street
Philadelphia, PA 19107
(215)567-7000

B.U.I.L.D., Inc.
(Broader Urban Involvement and Leadership Development)
1223 North Milwaukee Avenue
Chicago, IL 60622
(312)227-2880

For Further Reading

BOOKS

Barrett, Patti. *Too Busy to Clean? Over 500 Tips and Techniques to Make Housecleaning Easier.* Pownal, VT: Storey Communications, 1990.

Bingham, Mindy, and Stryker, Sandy. *More Choices: A Strategic Planning Guide for Mixing Career and Family.* Santa Barbara: Advocacy Press, 1987.

Booher, Diana Daniels. *Help! We're Moving.* New York: Julian Messner, 1978, 1983.

Bratman, Fred. *Everything You Need to Know When a Parent Dies.* New York: The Rosen Publishing Group, 1992.

Dolmetsch, Paul and Shih, Alexa (eds.). *The Kids' Book About Single-Parent Families.* New York: Doubleday and Company, 1985.

Feldman, Robert S. *Understanding Stress.* New York: Franklin Watts, 1992.

Goldman, Katherine Wyse. *My Mother Worked and I Turned Out Okay.* New York: Villard Books, 1993.

Gooden, Kimberly Wood. *Coping with Family Stress.* New York: The Rosen Publishing Group, 1989.

Grollman, Earl A. and Sweder, Gerri L. *The Working Parent Dilemma: How to Balance the Responsibilities of Children and Careers.* Boston: Benson Press, 1986.

Kalberg VanWie, Eileen. *Teenage Stress: How to Cope in a Complex World.* New York: Julian Messner, 1987.

Kleeberg, Irene Cumming. *Latch-Key Kid.* New York: Franklin Watts, 1985.

Kramer, Patricia. *Discovering Personal Goals.* (The Self-Esteem Library) New York: The Rosen Publishing Group, 1992.

Krementz, Jill. *How It Feels When a Parent Dies.* New York:

Alfred A. Knopf, 1981.

———. *How it Feels When Parents Divorce.* New York: Alfred A. Knopf, 1984.

Krueger, Caryl Waller. *Working Parent/Happy Child.* Nashville: Abingdon Press, 1990.

Kyte, Kathy S. *In Charge: A Complete Handbook for Kids with Working Parents.* New York: Alfred A. Knopf, 1983.

Lew, Irvina Siegel. *You Can't Do It All; Ideas That Work for Mothers Who Work.* New York: Atheneum, 1986.

Mason, Jerald W. *The Easy Family Budget.* Boston: Houghton Mifflin, 1990.

McCoy, Kathy. *The Teenage Survival Guide.* New York: Wallaby Books, 1981.

Murdock, Carol Vejvoda. *Single Parents Are People, Too!* New York: Butterick Publishing, 1980.

Nida, Patricia Cooney, Ph.D., and Heller, Wendy M. *The Teenager's Survival Guide to Moving.* New York: Atheneum, 1985.

Robson, Bonnie. *My Parents Are Divorced, Too: Teenagers Talk About Their Experiences and How They Cope.* New York: Everest House, 1980.

Roman, Beverly D. *Moving Minus Mishaps.* Bethlehem, PA: BR Anchor Publishing, 1991.

Ryan, Elizabeth A. *Straight Talk About Parents.* New York: Facts on File, 1989.

Salk, Dr. Lee. *Familyhood: Nurturing the Values That Matter.* New York: Simon and Schuster, 1992.

Smith, Sandra Lee. *Coping with Decision-Making,* rev. ed. New York: The Rosen Publishing Group, 1993.

St. Pierre, Stephanie. *Everything You Need to Know When a Parent Is in Jail.* New York: The Rosen Publishing Group, 1994.

Starer, Daniel. *Who to Call: The Parent's Source Book.* New York: Quill/Morrow, 1992.

Webb, Margot. Coping with Street Gangs, rev. ed. New York: The Rosen Publishing Group, 1995.

PAMPHLETS

Allstate Insurance Company. *Home Burglary: How Inviting Is Your Home?* 1993.

American National Red Cross. *Home Safety.* (Independent Living Series.) 1984.

Chicago Transit Authority. *CTA: Safer Than Ever; Tips for Safe Riding.*
Order from: CTA Marketing Department, Room 411
                    P.O. Box 3555
                    Merchandise Mart Plaza
                    Chicago, IL 60654
                    (312)664-7200, ext. 3316

League of Women Voters Education Fund. *Expanding School-Age Child Care: A Community Action Guide.*
Order from: League of Women Voters of the United States
                    1730 M Street N.W.
                    Washington, DC 20036

National Safety Council. *Child Alone.* 1985.

————. *Your Home Safety Checklist.* 1992.

Project Home Safe. *Preparing Your Child For Self-Care.* 1989.
For further information:
                    Project Home Safe
                    1555 King Street
                    Alexandria, VA 22314
                    (703)706-4600
                    (800)-252-SAFE

Index

DATE DUE
